HBR Guide to **Being More Productive**

Harvard Business Review Guides

Arm yourself with the advice you need to succeed on the job, from the most trusted brand in business. Packed with how-to essentials from leading experts, the HBR Guides provide smart answers to your most pressing work challenges.

The titles include:

HBR Guide to Being More Productive

HBR Guide to Better Business Writing

HBR Guide to Building Your Business Case

HBR Guide to Buying a Small Business

HBR Guide to Coaching Employees

HBR Guide to Data Analytics Basics for Managers

HBR Guide to Dealing with Conflict

HBR Guide to Delivering Effective Feedback

HBR Guide to Emotional Intelligence

HBR Guide to Finance Basics for Managers

HBR Guide to Getting the Right Work Done

HBR Guide to Giving Effective Feedback

HBR Guide to Leading Teams

HBR Guide to Making Every Meeting Matter

HBR Guide to Managing Up and Across

HBR Guide to Negotiating

HBR Guide to Office Politics

HBR Guide to Performance Management

HBR Guide to Persuasive Presentations

HBR Guide to Project Management

HBR Guide to
Being More Productive

HARVARD BUSINESS REVIEW PRESS

Boston, Massachusetts

Printed in the United States of America
10 9 8 7 6

Cataloging-in-Publication data is forthcoming.

ISBN: 978-1-63369-308-1
eISBN: 978-1-63369-309-8

The paper used in this publication meets the requirements of the American National Standard for Permanence of Paper for Publications and Documents in Libraries and Archives Z39.48-1992

MIX
Paper from responsible sources
FSC® C011935

What You'll Learn

Every day begins with the same challenge: too many tasks on your to-do list and not enough time to accomplish them. Perhaps you tell yourself to just buckle down and get it all done—skip lunch, work a longer day. Maybe you throw your hands up, recognize you can't do it all, and just begin fighting the biggest fire or greasing the squeakiest wheel.

And yet you know how good it feels on those days when you plow through your work—taking care of difficult and meaty projects while also knocking off the little things that have been hanging over your head forever. You made *real* progress on your work. Those times when your day didn't run you—you ran your day. To have more of those days more often, you need to discover what works for you: with your strengths, your preferences, and the things you *must* accomplish.

Whether you're an assistant or the CEO, whether you've been in the workforce for 40 years or are just starting out, this guide will help you be more productive.

You'll discover different ways to:

- Motivate yourself to work when you really don't want to
- Improve your focus
- Take on less, but get more done
- Preserve time for your most important work
- Set boundaries with colleagues—without alienating them
- Harness small pockets of time between meetings
- Take time off without tearing your hair out

Contents

SECTION ONE

Take Stock

1. Make Time for Work That Matters 3

Evaluate what's on your plate and then drop, delegate, or redesign.

BY JULIAN BIRKINSHAW AND JORDAN COHEN

2. Are You Too Stressed to Be Productive? Or Not Stressed Enough? 15

A research-based assessment.

BY FRANCESCA GINO

3. What's Your Personal Productivity Style? 25

How do you do your best work?

BY CARSON TATE

SECTION TWO

Plan Your Day

4. You May Hate Planning, but You Should Do It Anyway 35

The pain will be worth it.

BY ELIZABETH GRACE SAUNDERS

5. Making the Most of "Slow Time" 41
Get important work done, even when it's not urgent.
BY LYNDA CARDWELL

6. Align Your Time Management with Your Goals 47
A simple tool can help.

7. A Tool to Help You Reach Your Goals in Four Steps 53
Break them down and make a plan.
BY HEIDI GRANT

8. Sprints Are the Secret to Getting More Done 57
They're not just for software development.
BY JOHN ZERATSKY

9. Accomplish More by Committing to Less 63
What to consider before taking on a new project.
BY ELIZABETH GRACE SAUNDERS

10. How to Say No to Taking On More Work 71
But maintain relationships.
BY REBECCA KNIGHT

11. The Most Productive People Know Whom to Ignore 79
Not everything merits your time and attention.
BY ED BATISTA

12. Fending Off a Colleague Who Keeps Wasting Your Time 85
Traffic control for drive-by visitors.
BY DORIE CLARK

13. Give Yourself Permission to Work Fewer Hours 91
Without feeling guilty about it.
BY ELIZABETH GRACE SAUNDERS

14. You'll Feel Less Rushed If You Give Time Away 97
Research proves the paradox.
BY CASSIE MOGILNER

SECTION THREE

Find Your Focus

15. Five Ways to Minimize Office Distractions 105
Build your attention muscle.
BY JOSEPH GRENNY

16. Train Your Brain to Focus 111
You can learn to ignore distractions.
BY PAUL HAMMERNESS, MD, AND MARGARET MOORE

17. The Two Things Killing Your Ability to Focus 117
Devices and meetings.
BY WILLIAM TRESEDER

18. Faced with Distraction, We Need Willpower 123
Strengthen your self-control.
BY JOHN COLEMAN

19. How to Practice Mindfulness Throughout Your Workday 127
From when you wake up to your commute home.
BY RASMUS HOUGAARD AND JACQUELINE CARTER

20. Coffee Breaks Don't Boost Productivity After All 131

Take a meaningful microbreak.

BY CHARLOTTE FRITZ

21. Gazing at Nature Makes You More Productive: An Interview with Kate Lee 139

Forty seconds is all it takes.

BY NICOLE TORRES

22. Five Ways to Work from Home More Effectively 145

Log on and take charge of your day.

BY CAROLYN O'HARA

23. Things to Buy, Download, or Do When Working Remotely 153

Be productive no matter where you are.

BY ALEXANDRA SAMUEL

SECTION FOUR

Motivate Yourself

24. Finding Meaning at Work, Even When Your Job Is Dull 163

You don't need to be curing cancer to feel good about your job.

BY MORTEN HANSEN AND DACHER KELTNER

25. How to Make Yourself Work When You Just Don't Want To 169

Get that project off the back burner—for good.

BY HEIDI GRANT

26. How to Beat Procrastination 175

Outsmart your brain's tendency to put off big goals.

BY CAROLINE WEBB

27. Steps to Take When You're Starting to Feel Burned Out 181

Feeling overwhelmed is a signal, not a life sentence.

BY MONIQUE VALCOUR

28. Pronouns Matter When Psyching Yourself Up 187

Talk to yourself more effectively.

BY OZLEM AYDUK AND ETHAN KROSS

29. Staying Motivated When Everyone Else Is on Vacation 193

Take advantage of an empty office.

BY DORIE CLARK

SECTION FIVE

Get More Done on the Road

30. How to Use Your Travel Time Productively 199

Waiting in lines doesn't have to be a waste of time.

BY DORIE CLARK

31. How to Get Work Done on the Road 203

The hotel notepad: unsung productivity hero.

BY JOSEPH GRENNY

SECTION SIX

Take Time Off

32. Going on Vacation Doesn't Have to Stress You Out at Work 211

Ease your exit—and reentry.

BY ELIZABETH GRACE SAUNDERS

33. Don't Obsess Over Getting Everything Done Before a Vacation 217

A saner way to prepare for being out.

BY SCOTT EDINGER

34. Ease the Pain of Returning to Work After Time Off 223

Get back into the groove.

BY ALEXANDRA SAMUEL

Index 229

SECTION ONE

Take Stock

What's holding you back from feeling—and being—more effective at work? Do you squander your energy on busywork that you enjoy? Do you feel unable to cope with the sheer number of projects on your plate?

This section of the guide will help you assess yourself, to establish a baseline for what work you have to do, how stressed you are, and how you like to operate. Read all three articles and take all three assessments in this section in one sitting. Or choose just one, evaluate that aspect of yourself, and take what you've learned forward into another section of the guide. No matter which approach you choose, what you learn will inspire you to think about your work—and the way you're working—differently.

CHAPTER 1

Make Time for Work That Matters

by Julian Birkinshaw and Jordan Cohen

More hours in the day. It's one thing everyone wants, and yet it's impossible to attain. But what if you could free up significant time—maybe as much as 20% of your workday—to focus on the responsibilities that really matter?

We've spent the past three years studying how knowledge workers can become more productive and found that the answer is simple: Eliminate or delegate unimportant tasks and replace them with value-added ones.

Reprinted from *Harvard Business Review*, September 2013 (product #R1309K)

Our research indicates that knowledge workers spend a great deal of their time—an average of 41%—on discretionary activities that offer little personal satisfaction and could be handled competently by others. So why do they keep doing them? Because ridding oneself of work is easier said than done. We instinctively cling to tasks that make us feel busy and thus important, while our bosses, constantly striving to do more with less, pile on as many responsibilities as we're willing to accept.

We believe there's a way forward, however. Knowledge workers can make themselves more productive by thinking consciously about how they spend their time; deciding which tasks matter most to them and their organizations; and dropping or creatively outsourcing the rest. We tried this intervention with 15 executives at different companies, and they were able to dramatically reduce their involvement in low-value tasks: They cut desk work by an average of six hours a week and meeting time by an average of two hours a week. And the benefits were clear. For example, when Lotta Laitinen, a manager at If, a Scandinavian insurance company, jettisoned meetings and administrative tasks in order to spend more time supporting her team, it led to a 5% increase in sales by her unit over a three-week period.

While not everyone in our study was quite that successful, the results still astounded us. By simply asking knowledge workers to rethink and shift the balance of their work, we were able to help them free up nearly a fifth of their time—an average of one full day a week—and focus on more worthwhile tasks with the hours they saved.

Why It's So Hard

Knowledge workers present a real challenge to managers. The work they do is difficult to observe (since a lot of it happens inside their heads), and the quality of it is frequently subjective. A manager may suspect that an employee is spending her time inefficiently but be hard-pressed to diagnose the problem, let alone come up with a solution.

We interviewed 45 knowledge workers in 39 companies across eight industries in the United States and Europe to see how they spent their days. We found that even the most dedicated and impressive performers devoted large amounts of time to tedious, non-value-added activities such as desk work and "managing across" the organization (for example, meetings with people in other departments). These are tasks that the knowledge workers themselves rated as offering little personal utility and low value to the company (see sidebar "The Work That Knowledge Workers Do").

There are many reasons why this happens. Most of us feel entangled in a web of commitments from which it can be painful to extricate ourselves: We worry that we're letting our colleagues or employers down if we stop doing certain tasks. "I want to appear busy and productive—the company values team players," one participant observed. Also, those less important items on our to-do lists are not entirely without benefit. Making progress on any task—even an inessential one—increases our feelings of engagement and satisfaction, research has shown. And although meetings are widely derided as a

THE WORK THAT KNOWLEDGE WORKERS DO

Our research shows that desk-based work and "managing across" take up two-thirds of knowledge workers' time, on average . . .

Time spent on activities

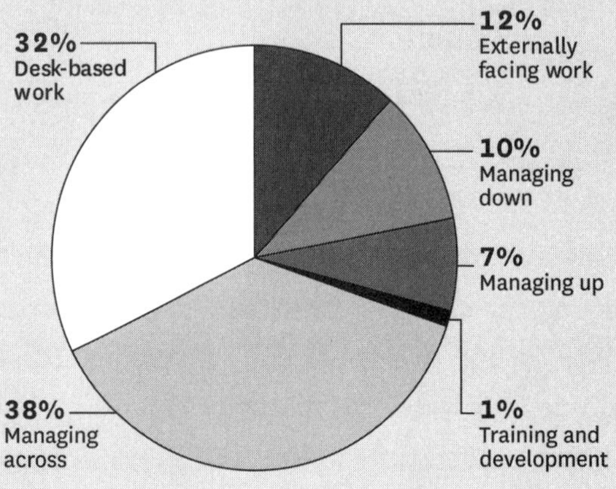

. . . and yet those tasks were rated as most easily off-loaded and tiresome.

Worth the time?

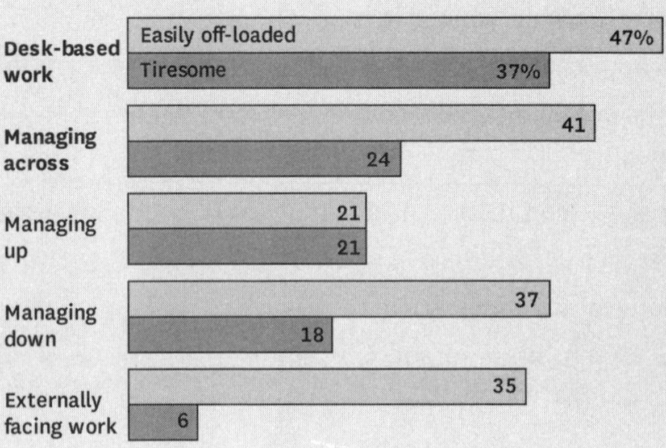

Armed with this knowledge, study participants dropped, delegated, outsourced, or postponed low-value tasks to free up time for more important work.

Time saved

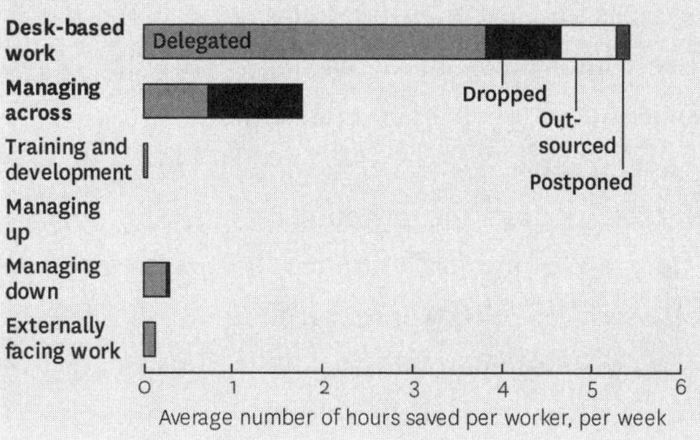

waste of time, they offer opportunities to socialize and connect with coworkers. "I actually quite look forward to face-to-face meetings," one respondent told us. "A call is more efficient, but it's a cold, lifeless medium."

Organizations share some of the blame for less-than-optimal productivity. Cost-cutting has been prevalent over the past decade, and knowledge workers, like most employees, have had to take on some low-value tasks—such as making travel arrangements—that distract them from more important work. Even though business confidence is rebounding, many companies are hesitant to add back resources, particularly administrative ones. What's more, increasingly complicated regulatory environments and tighter control systems in many industries have contributed to risk-averse corporate cultures that discourage senior people from ceding work to less seasoned colleagues. The consequences are predictable: "My team is understaffed and underskilled, so my calendar is a nightmare and I get pulled into many more meetings than I should," one study subject reported. Another commented, "I face the constraint of the working capacity of the people I delegate to."

Some companies do try to help their knowledge workers focus on the value-added parts of their job. For example, one of us (Jordan Cohen) helped Pfizer create a service called pfizerWorks, which allows employees to outsource less important tasks. We've also seen corporate initiatives that ban email on Fridays, put time limits on meetings, and forbid internal PowerPoint presentations. But it's very difficult to change institutional norms, and when knowledge workers don't buy in to such top-down directives, they find creative ways to resist or game the system, which only makes matters worse. We propose a sensible middle ground: judicious, self-directed interventions supported by management that help knowledge workers help themselves.

What Workers Can Do

Our process, a variant of the classic Start/Stop/Continue exercise, is designed to help you make small but significant changes to your day-to-day work schedule. We facilitated this exercise with the 15 executives mentioned above, and they achieved some remarkable results.

Identify low-value tasks

Using this self-assessment (see "Identifying Low-Value Tasks"), look at all your daily activities and decide which ones are (a) not that important to either you or your firm and (b) relatively easy to drop, delegate, or outsource. Our research suggests that at least one-quarter of a typical knowledge worker's activities fall into both categories, so you should aim to find up to 10 hours of time per week. The participants in our study pinpointed a range of expendable tasks. Lotta Laitinen, the manager at If, quickly identified several meetings and routine administrative tasks she could dispense with. Shantanu Kumar, CEO of a small technology company in London, realized he was too involved in project planning details, while Vincent Bryant, a manager at GDF SUEZ Energy Services, was surprised to see how much time he was wasting in sorting documents.

Decide whether to drop, delegate, or redesign

Sort the low-value tasks into three categories: *quick kills* (things you can stop doing now with no negative effects), *off-load opportunities* (tasks that can be delegated with minimal effort), and *long-term redesign* (work that needs to be restructured or overhauled). Our study participants found that this step forced them to reflect carefully on their real contributions to their respective organizations. "I took a step back and asked myself, 'Should I be doing this in the first place? Can my subordinate do it? Is he up to it?'" recalls Johann Barchechath, a manager at BNP Paribas. "This helped me figure out what

SELF-ASSESSMENT: IDENTIFYING LOW-VALUE TASKS

Make a list of everything you did yesterday or the day before, divided into 30- or 60-minute chunks. For each task, ask yourself four questions:

How valuable is this activity to the firm?

Suppose you're updating your boss or a senior executive on your performance. Would you mention this task? Would you be able to justify spending time on it?

	SCORE
It contributes in a significant way toward the company's overall objectives.	4
It contributes in a small way.	3
It has no impact, positive or negative.	2
It has a negative impact.	1

To what extent could I let this go?

Imagine that because of a family emergency, you arrive at work two hours late and have to prioritize the day's activities. Which category would this activity fall in?

Essential: This takes top priority.	4
Important: I need to get this done today.	3
Discretionary: I'll get to it if time allows.	2
Unimportant/optional: I can cut this immediately.	1

How much personal value do I get from doing it?

Imagine that you're financially independent and creating your dream job. Would you keep this task or jettison it?

Definitely keep: It's one of the best parts of my job.	5
Probably keep: I enjoy this activity.	4
Not sure: This task has good and bad points.	3
Probably drop: I find this activity somewhat tiresome.	2
Definitely jettison: I dislike doing it.	1

To what extent could someone else do it on my behalf?

Suppose you've been tapped to handle a critical, fast-track initiative and have to assign some of your work to colleagues for three months. Would you drop, delegate, or keep this task?

Only I (or someone senior to me) can handle this task.	5
This task is best done by me because of my particular skill set and other, linked responsibilities.	4
If structured properly, this task could be handled satisfactorily by someone junior to me.	3
This task could easily be handled by a junior employee or outsourced to a third party.	2
This task could be dropped altogether.	1

Tally your score

A low total score (10 or lower) reflects a task that is a likely candidate for delegation or elimination.	☐

was valuable for the bank versus what was valuable for me—and what we simply shouldn't have been doing at all." Another participant noted, "I realized that the big change I should make is to say no up front to low-value tasks and not commit myself in the first place."

Off-load tasks

We heard from many participants that delegation was initially the most challenging part—but ultimately very rewarding. One participant said he couldn't stop worrying about the tasks he had reassigned, while another told us he had trouble remembering "to push, prod, and chase." Barchechath observed, "I learned about the importance of timing in delegating something—it is possible to delegate too early."

Most participants eventually overcame those stumbling blocks. They delegated from 2% to 20% of their work with no decline in their productivity or their team's. "I overestimated my subordinate's capability at first, but it got easier after a while, and even having a partially done piece of work created energy for me," Barchechath said. A bonus was that junior employees benefited from getting more involved. "[She] told me several times that she really appreciated it," he added. Vincent Bryant decided to off-load tasks to a virtual personal assistant and says that although he was concerned about getting up to speed with the service, "it was seamless."

Allocate freed-up time

The goal, of course, is to be not just efficient but effective. So the next step is to determine how to best make use of the time you've saved. Write down two or three things you should be doing but aren't, and then keep a log to assess whether you're using your time more effectively. Some of our study participants were able to go home a bit earlier to enjoy their families (which probably made them happier and more productive the next day). Some unfortunately reported that their time was immediately swallowed up by unforeseen events: "I cleared my inbox and found myself firefighting."

But more than half reclaimed the extra hours to do better work. "For me the most useful part was identifying the important things I don't get time for usually," Kumar said. "I stopped spending time with my project planning tool and instead focused on strategic activities, such as the product road map." Laitinen used her freed-up schedule to listen in on client calls, observe her top salespeople, and coach her employees one-on-one. The result was that stunning three-week sales jump of 5%, with the biggest increases coming from below-average performers. A questionnaire showed that employee responses to the experiment were positive, and Laitinen found that she missed nothing by dropping some of her work. "The first week was really stressful, because I had to do so much planning, but by the middle of the test period, I was more relaxed, and I was satisfied when I went home every day."

Commit to your plan

Although this process is entirely self-directed, it's crucial to share your plan with a boss, colleague, or mentor. Explain which activities you are getting out of and why. And agree to discuss what you've achieved in a few weeks' time. Without this step, it's all too easy to slide back into bad habits. Many of our participants found that their managers were helpful and supportive. Laitinen's boss, Sven Kärnekull suggested people to whom she could delegate her work. Other participants discovered that simply voicing the commitment to another person helped them follow through. With relatively little effort and no management directive, the small intervention we propose can significantly boost productivity among knowledge workers. Such shifts are not always easy, of course. "It's hard to make these changes without the discipline of someone standing over you," one of our study participants remarked. But all agreed that the exercise was a useful "forcing mechanism" to help them become more efficient, effective, and engaged employees and managers. To do the same, you don't have to redesign any parts of an organization, reengineer a work process, or transform a business model. All you have to do is ask the right questions and act on the answers. After all, if you're a knowledge worker, isn't using your judgment what you were hired for?

Julian Birkinshaw is a professor of strategy and entrepreneurship at London Business School. **Jordan Cohen** is Head of Organizational Effectiveness, Learning & Development and Talent at Weight Watchers International. He is an expert on knowledge worker productivity and is a frequent contributor to HBR.

CHAPTER 2

Are You Too Stressed to Be Productive? Or Not Stressed Enough?

by Francesca Gino

If you're like me, you often ask yourself how you can get more work done in a day. How can you best boost your productivity? I always assumed that if I could just reduce any stress I was facing, my productivity would rise. But my intuition was, in fact, wrong. It's true that stress can be a health risk, and that we're often encouraged to

---

Adapted from content posted on hbr.org on April 14, 2016

FIGURE 2-1

The Yerkes-Dodson Law

How anxiety affects performance.

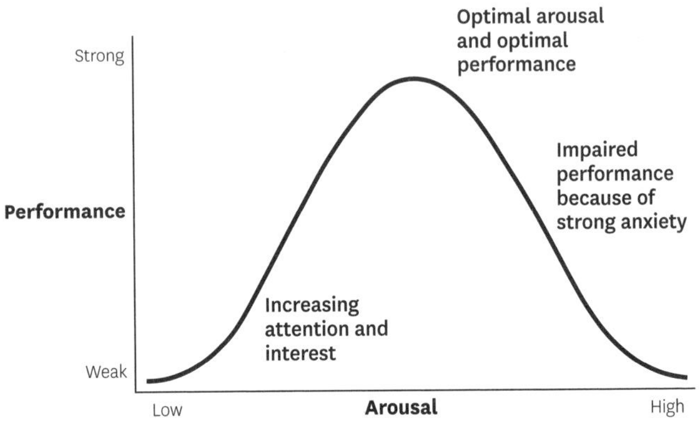

Source: Robert M. Yerkes and John D. Dodson

avoid it if we want to live happy, productive, and long lives. But research suggests that some stress can actually be beneficial to performance.

Take a look at figure 2-1. According to what is known as the "Yerkes-Dodson law," performance increases with physiological or mental arousal (stress) but only up to a point. When the level of stress becomes too high, performance decreases.

There's more: The shape of the curve varies based on the complexity and familiarity of the task. Different tasks require different levels of arousal for optimal performance, research has found. For example, difficult or unfamiliar tasks require lower levels of arousal to facilitate concentration; by contrast, you may better perform tasks demanding stamina or persistence with higher levels of arousal to induce and increase motivation.

Given this relationship between stress and performance, it's probably beneficial to understand how much stress you're currently experiencing at work. If you're curious, see the sidebar "How Stressed Are You?" to take an assessment (which is adapted from the commonly used Perceived Stress Scale, created by Sheldon Cohen, Tom Kamarck, and Robin Mermelstein).

Higher scores, as you might guess, correspond to higher levels of stress. Based on my use of this test in executive education classrooms and in research conducted with other groups, scores around 13 are considered average. Usually, scores in this range indicate that your attention and interest are at the proper level, allowing you to be productive at work. Referring to the Yerkes-Dodson law, such scores generally correspond to an optimal level of arousal and thus performance.

But if your score is much higher or much lower, you're likely experiencing stress in a way that is detrimental to productivity. In particular, scores of 20 or more are generally considered to indicate an unproductive level of stress. But even scores that indicate low levels of stress—commonly, scores of 4 or lower—could be problematic since they signal an insufficient level of arousal to keep you engaged in your work. If this is the case, try to find healthy ways of raising your stress by taking on more challenging tasks or responsibilities. Increasing stress may feel counterintuitive, but according to research by Sheldon Cohen and Denise Janicki-Deverts (published in the *Journal of Applied Social Psychology*), increasing

HOW STRESSED ARE YOU?

When answering these questions, focus on your thoughts and feelings during the last month. For an interactive version of this assessment and to see how your score compares with other hbr.org readers, visit https://hbr.org/2016/04/are-you-too-stressed-to-be-productive-or-not-stressed-enough.

	Very often (4 points)	Fairly often (3 points)	Sometimes (2 points)	Almost never (1 point)	Never (0 points)
1. In the last month, how often have you been upset because of something that happened unexpectedly?					
2. How often have you felt unable to control the important things in your life?					
3. How often have you felt nervous and stressed?					
4. How often have you felt confident about your ability to handle your personal problems?					
5. How often have you felt that things were going your way?					

	Very often (4 points)	Fairly often (3 points)	Some-times (2 points)	Almost never (1 point)	Never (0 points)	
6. How often have you felt unable to cope with all the things that you had to do?						
7. How often have you been able to control irritations in your life?						
8. How often have you felt on top of things?						
9. How often have you felt angry because of things that were outside your control?						
10. How often have you felt that difficul-ties were piling up so high that you could not overcome them?						Total score
Total						

Add your total points in each column and then tally the numbers in the last row to find your total score.

If your total score is . . .

- Around 13, that's average, and a good amount of stress to be productive without being overwhelmed
- Much lower than average, around 4, then perhaps you're not experiencing *enough* stress to be engaged
- Much higher than average, 25 or above, then your stress level is probably detrimental to your productivity—and your health

FIGURE 2-2

Average stress levels by gender, age, education, and income

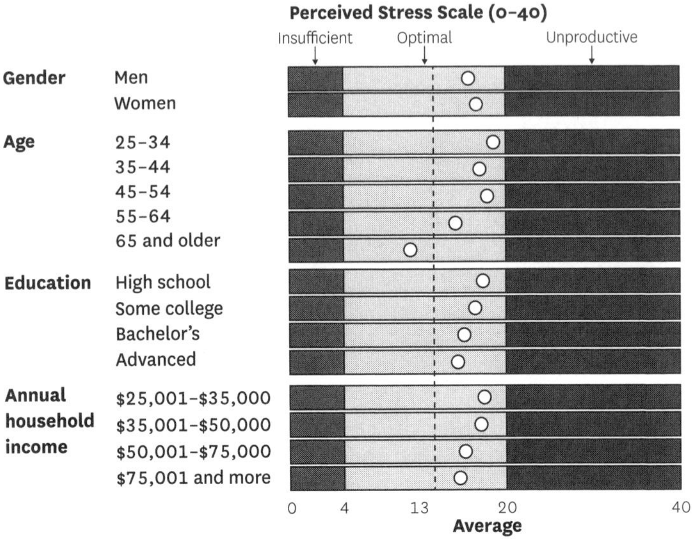

Source: Sheldon Cohen and Denise Janicki-Deverts

arousal also corresponds to increasing attention and interest (up to a point).

For comparison, here are some average scores from research conducted using the scale in figure 2-2:

If your score approaches or exceeds 20, here are some strategies that may help you reduce stress to a more productive level:

Increase your control. One simple solution to lowering stress is to find more ways to increase your control over the work you do. People tend to believe that high-level positions bring a lot of stress, but research suggests just the opposite: Leaders with higher levels of responsibility experience lower stress levels than those with less on their shoulders. This is because leaders have more control over their activities. Independent of where you sit in the organizational hierarchy, you may have ways to increase your sense of control—namely, by focusing on aspects of your work where you can make choices (for example, choosing one project over another or simply choosing the order in which you answer emails).

Find more opportunities to be authentic. Evidence suggests that people often experience feelings of inauthenticity at work. That is, they conform to the opinions of colleagues rather than voicing their own, and they go with others' flow rather than setting their own agenda. This, my research suggests, has important implications for your stress level and performance. When people behave in inauthentic ways, they experience higher levels of anxiety than when they are simply themselves. So, try to find ways to express who you are at work, such as offering to share your unique talents or decorating your office to reflect who you are.

Use rituals. Basketball superstar Michael Jordan wore his University of North Carolina shorts underneath his Chicago Bulls shorts at every game; Curtis Martin, former running back of the New York Jets, read Psalm 91 before every game; and Wade Boggs, as third baseman for the Boston Red Sox, ate chicken before each game and took batting practice at exactly

5:17 p.m., fielded exactly 117 ground balls, and ran sprints at precisely 7:17 p.m. These rituals may sound strange, but they can actually improve performance.

In one recent experiment, people asked to hit a golf ball into a hole received either a so-called "lucky" golf ball or an ordinary golf ball. In another experiment, participants performing a motor dexterity task (placing 36 small balls in 36 holes by tilting the plastic cube containing them) were either asked to simply start the game or heard the researcher say they would cross their fingers for them. The superstitious rituals enhanced people's confidence in their abilities, motivated greater effort—and improved subsequent performance.

Similarly, research in sports psychology demonstrates the benefits of pre-performance routines, from improving attention and execution to increasing emotional stability and confidence. And recently, my colleagues and I have found that when people engage in rituals before undertaking high-stakes tasks, they feel less anxious and stressed about the task and end up performing better as a result.

A moderate amount of stress may put you in the right mindset to tackle your work. But if you're feeling overwhelmed, I hope you'll try out some of these strategies to not only improve your productivity but also increase your happiness.

Francesca Gino is the Tandon Family Professor of Business Administration at Harvard Business School, a faculty affiliate of the Behavioral Insights Group at Harvard Kennedy School, and the author of *Sidetracked: Why Our Decisions Get Derailed, and How We Can Stick to the Plan* (Harvard Business Review Press, 2013). She cochairs an HBS executive education program on applying behavioral economics to organizational problems. Follow her on Twitter: @francescagino.

CHAPTER 3

What's Your Personal Productivity Style?

by Carson Tate

When it comes to personal productivity advice, one size doesn't fit all. In fact, your cognitive style—that is, the way you prefer to perceive and process information—can have a dramatic impact on the success or failure of time management techniques and performance enhancement strategies. This assessment is designed to help you understand your own style—how you think, learn, and communicate best—and to guide you toward productivity tips that like-minded people have found most effective.

Adapted from content posted on hbr.org on January 26, 2015

Take Stock

In table 3-1, indicate how often each statement applies to you.

TABLE 3-1

Determine your productivity style

	1 Never	2 Rarely	3 Sometimes	4 Often	5 Always
1. I use a prioritized list to complete my work.					
2. I'm late to meetings and appointments.					
3. When I plan a project, I first think about who needs to be involved.					
4. When I brainstorm, I sketch or draw my ideas.					
5. I complete work quickly.					
6. I have trouble saying no to my colleagues.					
7. I plan for the next day.					
8. Daydreaming helps me solve important problems.					
9. In project meetings, I'm able to synthesize disparate ideas.					
10. I prefer to work on a team.					
11. I use step-by-step project plans.					
12. I honor deadlines.					
13. I do my best work under pressure.					
14. I block off time on my calendar to complete work.					

	1 Never	2 Rarely	3 Sometimes	4 Often	5 Always
15. I analyze a project before I start it.					
16. I use established routines and systems to complete tasks.					
17. When I brainstorm, I list my ideas.					
18. I eliminate physical clutter in my office.					
19. When I plan a project, I first think about how it supports the strategic vision of my team or organization.					
20. It's hard for me to take time for leisure when there's still work to do.					
21. I designate specific times of the day for certain tasks.					
22. I complete project tasks in sequence.					
23. I accurately complete significant amounts of work.					
24. I tend to underestimate how long it will take to complete tasks and projects.					
25. When I plan a project, I first think about the required project deliverables.					
26. I'm selective about the tools—pens, paper, folders, and so on—that I use.					
27. When I brainstorm, I talk to others about my ideas.					
28. When I plan a project, I first think about the goal to be achieved.					

(*continued*)

TABLE 3-1 *(continued)*

Productivity Style Assessment® Scoring

Add your scores for the items listed in each column. The column with the highest score is your primary Productivity Style.

1 = ______	7 = ______	3 = ______	2 = ______
15 = ______	11 = ______	6 = ______	4 = ______
17 = ______	12 = ______	10 = ______	5 = ______
20 = ______	16 = ______	14 = ______	8 = ______
21 = ______	18 = ______	24 = ______	9 = ______
23 = ______	22 = ______	26 = ______	13 = ______
28 = ______	25 = ______	27 = ______	19 = ______
Total Prioritizer: ________	Total Planner: ________	Total Arranger: ________	Total Visualizer: ________

The Four Productivity Styles

Prioritizers

Prioritizers prefer logical, analytical, fact-based, critical, and realistic thinking. They use time effectively and focus on the highest-value tasks, accurately completing significant amounts of work. They analyze project goals and strive to achieve the desired outcomes.

Productivity tools that appeal to Prioritizers include:

- The iPad (which they can customize to streamline their work flow)
- Productivity apps that allow them to log into their devices anywhere and complete work remotely like Evernote, Noteshelf, To Do, LogMeIn Ignition

- ScanBizCards, which lets them scan business cards on the run
- Classic low-tech tools like legal pads and label makers

Prioritizers will especially enjoy chapter 6, "Align Your Time Management with Your Goals," and chapter 7, "A Tool to Help You Reach Your Goals in Four Steps."

Planners

Planners prefer organized, sequential, and detailed thinking. They create to-do lists, set aside time for tasks, and prepare thorough and accurate project plans. They don't waste time on anything unproductive or unimportant. They comply with laws, policies, regulations, and quality and safety criteria, and they frequently complete work ahead of deadline.

Productivity tools that appeal to Planners include:

- Digital lists and project planning apps that let them create and track their work by project, place, person, or date like Tom's Planner and OmniFocus
- Agendas, which lets them create interactive agendas and broadcast them to iPad users
- ZipList, which creates both personal and shared family shopping lists, organizing items both by category and by the store that carries them
- Low-tech tools like label makers, file folders, filing cabinets, drawer organizers, pen holders, and other office organizational supplies

Planners may want to start by reading chapter 9, "Accomplish More by Committing to Less," and chapter 10, "How to Say No to Taking On More Work."

Arrangers

Arrangers prefer supportive, expressive, and emotional thinking. They encourage teamwork to maximize output, and they make decisions intuitively as events unfold. They block off time to complete work but excel at partnering with others to get it done. They communicate effectively, which helps them build and lead project teams. They tend to maintain visual lists, often using color.

Productivity tools that appeal to Arrangers include:

- Dictation apps like Dragon NaturallySpeaking and Dragon Dictation or the web-based program Copytalk
- Collaboration tools like GoToMeeting, WebEx, SharePlus Office Mobile Client, and Join.me
- Aesthetically pleasing office supplies—for example, notebooks with unlined pages and pens in a variety of ink colors

Arrangers will enjoy chapter 14, "You'll Feel Less Rushed If You Give Time Away," and chapter 29, "Staying Motivated When Everyone Else Is on Vacation."

Visualizers

Visualizers prefer holistic, intuitive, integrative thinking. They manage and juggle multiple tasks while still seeing the big picture. They're known for creativity and innovation and for synthesizing others' disparate ideas into a cohesive whole. They think strategically about projects and work quickly to execute tasks. They tend to maintain visual lists, often using color.

Productivity tools that appeal to Visualizers include:

- Digital whiteboard apps
- SketchBook Pro, an app that lets them capture ideas while working with a complete set of sketching and painting tools
- iThoughts HD, a digital mind-mapping tool
- Concur, an app used to photograph and save expense receipts and create expense reports
- Noteshelf, a digital notebook tool
- Visually vibrant low-tech tools such as multicolored Post-it notes, colored folders, notebooks with unlined pages, pens in a variety of ink colors, large whiteboards, baskets, folders, and bags and clipboards for keeping papers visible and organized.

Visualizers may benefit from reading chapter 8, "Sprints Are the Secret to Getting More Done," and chapter 21, "Gazing at Nature Makes You More Productive."

Carson Tate is an expert on workplace productivity and the author of *Work Simply: Embracing the Power of Your Personal Productivity Style.*

SECTION TWO

Plan Your Day

Every day is a new opportunity to get it right. To do more and do it more efficiently. To feel better about the work you're doing.

Evaluate the tasks you have to do today, set priorities, and make a plan for getting your most important work accomplished with the advice in this section of the guide.

CHAPTER 4

You May Hate Planning, but You Should Do It Anyway

by Elizabeth Grace Saunders

Some of the smartest people that I have ever met struggle with convincing themselves to do one thing: plan their work.

They're off the charts in terms of analyzing all sorts of things, from manufacturing processes to stocks to nuclear particles. But when it comes to their own time management or laying out a plan to get a big project done, they balk. Something about scheduling makes

---

Adapted from content posted on hbr.org on September 19, 2016

their brains shut down, and they can go from brilliant to blank in an instant.

One of the reasons these individuals struggle is because they can get away with not planning for much longer than most people. If you have some charisma and a strong ability to cram, you may have been able to pull off decent work at the last minute—or at least find ways to get an extension. If you can continue in this way without any major issues, there's no need to change.

But as time demands increase—you get a new job, you're short-staffed, you get married or have kids, or your health changes—a life without planning or routines can make you tired at best and miserable at worst. At some point, you need to decide that it's worth the time and effort to create plans and routines. Based on my experience with time management clients, here are some tough truths about planning that every individual needs to accept before moving forward. Once you accept them and make planning a habit, you can harness its power to create a happier, healthier, and more productive life.

Planning Will Trigger Pain—at Least Initially

If you have very weak planning patterns in your brain, you will literally feel pain when you begin to plan. It's like when you start a new exercise routine and work out muscles that you didn't even know you had. But as you develop the habit of planning, the pain associated with it usually decreases. And the more positive reinforcement you get, the more you do it.

For example, Camille Fournier, former CTO of Rent the Runway, described the pain and reward of planning (in an Ask the CTO column on O'Reilly.com). She faced stress and frustration when she first began planning her projects, explaining how her boss would dissect her plans—wherever there was uncertainty or risk—and ask her to go back and reconsider it. "It was absolutely dreadful," she said, "and I found myself deeply frustrated and impatient throughout the process. And yet, at the end of it all, we broke this big project down into deliverable chunks, and I went on to successfully lead a significant architectural change that ran close to the schedule, despite its complexity. The memory of the frustration of planning is burned into my brain, but so is the memory of the huge accomplishment that came out of that planning."

In some cases, planning works best when you don't have to go it alone. Consider planning a major project as a team or at least with one other person. Depending on the size of the team and the overlap of the work, breaking down monthly goals into a weekly plan together can make the process easier.

Planning Takes Longer Than Expected (and So Does the Work)

Planning your week typically takes 30–60 minutes, and project planning takes much longer. For those unfamiliar with planning, this amount of time can seem excessive. But those who have seen its power understand that one hour a week can make hundreds of hours of thoughtful work less stressful and more productive.

What's more, part of the benefit of planning is that you gain greater clarity on how long work actually takes versus how long you thought it would take. This can lead to some more frustration initially because you have to face the fact that the reality is different from what you hoped. Planning also doesn't mean that everything will go according to schedule. But it does allow you to know early on if something goes off course, so you can do something about it, rather than getting stuck with little or no options later.

Things Tend to Go Better When You Plan

When you plan, you'll often discover some hard truths about what it will take to accomplish a project or simply get your work done this week. You may feel a bit uncomfortable because you're no longer in a pleasant, imaginary world where there's an infinite amount of time, and you can get everything done all at once and make everyone happy. But discovering these facts as early as possible gives you the ability to quickly negotiate expectations on deliverables or pull in more resources on a project. You can confidently set boundaries and decide what you're going to do for the day because you're aware of your full array of options and the current priorities. This maximizes your effectiveness and allows you to consistently set and meet expectations.

Planning Becomes the Canary

In the past, miners brought canaries into mines as an early-detection warning system. If the canaries died, it was a sign that the toxic gases were rising and the miners needed to get out. Planning can provide the same sort of early warning signals—if you veer significantly off your estimated plan, it's a sign that something is wrong and you need to make adjustments. Having a plan and checking against it allow you to make those adjustments before your projects or other time commitments are in major peril.

Many individuals who don't like to plan tend to abandon planning quickly, assuming that they have things under control. But that sends them in a downward spiral. Keeping an eye on the plan and making adjustments is just as important as delivering a complete product—it maintains process stability. If you ignore the canary, you have a greater chance of failing, just because you didn't notice important signs.

Can planning be difficult? Yes. But is it possible for you to do more of it? Absolutely. The payoff of going through the pain of planning can be huge in terms of increased productivity, decreased stress, and, most of all, intentional alignment with what's most important.

Elizabeth Grace Saunders is the author of *How to Invest Your Time Like Money* (Harvard Business Review Press, 2015), a time coach, and the founder of Real Life E Time Coaching & Training. Find out more at www.RealLifeE.com.

CHAPTER 5

Making the Most of "Slow Time"

by Lynda Cardwell

Years ago, when Fannie Mae's public finance business was added to the work portfolio for Wayne Curtis, vice president of partnership investments, he had to fundamentally rethink his approach to work. Before, an agreement to extend a line of credit to a state or local authority for a 50-unit housing project might crystallize over a two-month period. But now, on top of this responsibility was the fast-paced work involved in evaluating multi-billion-dollar bond purchases.

"Suddenly, my business volume had increased by a factor of 10," he says, "and the rhythm of the new work

---

Adapted from content posted on hbr.org on February 28, 2008

was very different from the work I had been doing. I was really grappling with how to stay focused on long-term priorities." An additional challenge was one faced by many of us when we become managers: the expectation that we'll continue to perform as technical experts even though our primary duties are now managerial and strategic. This creates the tendency to hold on to tasks that our direct reports could handle.

Dilemmas like these highlight the way that the pace and pressure of work crowd out what author Thomas Hylland Eriksen calls "slow time." Being able to work faster and to take on more work is jeopardizing our high performance. Increasingly we find ourselves with little—if any—of the kind of time ideally suited for the detailed, focused, and unhurried intellectual and interpersonal work upon which high performance depends, he explains in *Tyranny of the Moment.*

How do you make the most of this precious commodity? For some time, management experts have advised that you develop an understanding of the interplay between importance and urgency in the tasks you face. More recent thinking, however, underscores the importance of recognizing the rhythm associated with a given task.

Triaging the Tasks You Face

To maximize your slow time, you have to be clear about your purpose, says Washington, DC–based executive coach David Coleman. "Key things you want to accomplish go into your schedule first, so that everything else falls in line." Using a technique from the classic time-management book *First Things First*, by Stephen A. Covey et al., Coleman has his clients imagine that they have rocks, gravel, and sand with which to fill a bowl. The rocks represent the most strategically significant tasks; the gravel, the work that has the next highest priority; and the sand, the least important activities.

Starting with the sand and gravel leaves no room for the rocks. But by working backward—starting with rocks first, then putting in the gravel, and finally adding the sand—clients find that there's plenty of room for everything. The highest-priority goals get first crack at a client's time, and the other tasks get accomplished in descending order of importance. Suddenly, the once overwhelming to-do list seems very doable. Many management experts suggest using a simple two-by-two matrix to identify your highest-priority tasks. *First Things First* defines the four quadrants in such a matrix as:

1. **Urgent and important tasks (Quadrant I).** For example, dealing with a product recall or completing due diligence before an acquisition can be approved.

2. **Not urgent but important tasks (Quadrant II).** Examples here include developing key business relationships and drafting a plan for how your company will respond to the changes you foresee taking place in your industry 18 months down the road.

3. **Urgent but not important tasks (Quadrant III).** Examples of these tasks are taking impromptu

phone calls from sales reps or fielding a request from a colleague to help make arrangements for next week's unit party.

4. **Not urgent and not important tasks (Quadrant IV).** For instance, surfing the internet or chatting with colleagues.

For this discussion, Quadrant II is the most significant because it represents the activities that call for slow time. Bethesda, Maryland–based executive coach Catherine Fitzgerald says that when her clients use this two-by-two matrix, "it's like a light bulb going off." They see that valuable time is being wasted on urgent but not important tasks instead of being spent on those that are important. Fitzgerald advises her clients to block out time every day for the important but not urgent work. One focus of this time should be coaching your team to take on responsibilities that are not essential for you to do yourself but that you often hang onto out of a sense of duty.

"You can easily free up at least 5% of your most valuable time by handing off things," she says. "And those tasks often prove to be interesting to a direct report."

Identifying the Rhythms

The more time you devote to important but not urgent work, the more control you have over your schedule. In particular, your time will less likely be consumed by putting out fires. This comes as no big surprise—so why is it, then, that people have so much difficulty reducing the time they spend on urgent but unimportant tasks?

Stephan Rechtschaffen, author of *Timeshifting*, believes the answer has to do with a process known as entrainment, in which a person becomes almost psychologically addicted to the rhythm of the particular task they're performing.

"When you get to tasks that are not urgent and not important, something really interesting happens," Rechtschaffen observes. "The ambient rhythm in modern life is so fast that even in our leisure time, instead of relaxing, we tend to take on activities that keep us in this fast rhythm." Thus, typical Quadrant IV recreational activities tend to be things like watching television (with its fast cuts and high-energy commercials) or playing video games (in which the action moves very rapidly).

"Once you're in a rhythm, the tendency is to stay in synchronization with that rhythm," says Rechtschaffen. The result is that "in modern life, Quadrant I, III, and IV activities are all happening at high frequencies. Even though the way to reduce the number of Quadrant I crises in your life is to spend more time in Quadrant II, people resist going there because its rhythm is so different."

To concentrate on work that is important but not urgent, you have to learn how to gear down. Rechtschaffen recommends scheduling specific times for such tasks. "I set aside time for doing my writing. The ground rule is that although I don't actually have to be writing during this time, I can't do anything else. What I've found, as I'm sitting there not writing, is that guilt feelings or feelings of inadequacy as a writer come up.

"I think this happens to many people who are attempting to do important but not urgent work: They're reluctant to face the feelings that surface when they slow down. The feelings hijack us; they act as perpetual motion machines, preventing us from comfortably entering into the activity. So instead of sitting with the feelings of guilt or inadequacy, we flee into high-frequency tasks."

The only way out of this trap, says Rechtschaffen, is to acknowledge the feelings that come up when you try to slow down—to let them "rise and then fall like a wave." Pausing after you finish a high-frequency task and before you begin Quadrant II work can help you consciously shift gears, he points out, as can putting on slow, classical music or doing a few minutes of breathing exercises designed to promote mindfulness.

"It's not so much the outer management of time that's important as it is the inner management," says Rechtschaffen. "The fundamental error lies in getting so entrained to a particular rhythm that you can't engage in the task at hand, whether it's a fast-paced activity or a slow-paced one, in a fully present way."

Lynda Cardwell is a marketing writer and publicist based in Birmingham, Alabama.

CHAPTER 6

Align Your Time Management with Your Goals

What goals are you aiming for in your work? Does the way that you're spending your time actually correlate to those goals? Without answers to these questions, you won't know how the many tasks on your list should be prioritized, organized, and ultimately accomplished. At the end of a busy day, sometimes it's hard to figure out where the time went. The following simple process will help you prioritize your work and understand how you're actually using your time.

Adapted from *Getting Work Done* (20-Minute Manager; product #14003), Harvard Business Review Press, 2014

List Your Goals

Ideally, you and your manager should meet at the start of each year to formulate a set of performance goals. From your discussion, you should understand how those goals tie into the company's aims and mission. You likely also have your own personal career goals. Together, these may look something like, "Improve people-management skills. Manage six new products. Handle contracts for all of the department's new products. Develop vendor-management skills."

Revisiting them now, write these goals down—on paper or in a note-taking app if you prefer. You will use these goals in two ways: first, to prioritize your daily work; and second, to gauge your progress (in other words, to benchmark what you're accomplishing and whether the changes you make as a result of reading this book are effective for you). By referring back to this list regularly, you'll identify which tasks are most important for you to tackle so you can plan accordingly.

Track Your Time

Once you've identified your goals, examine how you're currently spending your time. Are you working on the things you *should* be doing—the things that will allow you to reach those goals—or are you getting bogged down by unrelated tasks or unexpected crises?

In order to truly understand where you're spending your time and to identify whether you should adjust your workload, track your work for two weeks by completing the following exercise. You may discover that your results don't align with your goals. The point is to uncover where that misalignment occurs so you can correct it.

First, write down your activities

Consider this a brain dump and include everything. List all of the tasks you perform, meetings you attend, and even the time you spend socializing or procrastinating at work. Look back over your calendar for the last week or two to get a sense of the range of your activities. Once you have a full list, break it down into broad categories so you can track the amount of time you spend doing tasks in each category. Some categories to consider include:

Core responsibilities: day-to-day tasks that make up the crux of your job

Personal growth: activities and projects that you find meaningful and valuable, but may not be part of your everyday responsibilities

Managing people: your work with others, including direct reports, colleagues, and even your superiors

Crises and fires: interruptions and urgent matters that arise occasionally and unexpectedly

Free time: lunch breaks and time spent writing personal emails, browsing the web, or checking social media

Administrative tasks: necessary tasks that you perform each day, such as approving time sheets or invoices, or putting together expense reports

Seeing your work broken into categories like this will help you visualize how you're really spending your time, and you may already be getting a sense of whether this lines up with the goals you identified.

Then, track your time

Once you have established your categories, begin tracking how much time you spend doing tasks in each. Estimate by the hour, or if you want to dig deeper into your habits, you can get more granular. To record your results, use either an online time-tracking tool or a standard calendar; to analyze those results, use a spreadsheet like the one depicted in table 6-1. List each category in its own column, and write the days of the week in each row. Calculate the time you spend on each task for each category for the next two weeks and put the totals in the corresponding categories.

At this point, you may be thinking, "I'm busy; I don't have time to log everything I do." It's true: This system does require an up-front investment of time and effort.

But logging your tasks and how long it takes to complete them will let you clearly see where you're spending too much time and where you need to begin to reallocate time to achieve your goals. If you want to improve your people-management skills, for example, you may realize that devoting 10 hours a week is not enough; perhaps you need to offload some administrative tasks so you have the additional time you need for that goal. By making small, deliberate shifts in how you spend your day, you'll ensure that you're investing the right amount of time on the tasks that matter most, making you more efficient at achieving your goals.

TABLE 6-1

Sample chart for tracking time spent on tasks per week

Week ending 4/14	Core responsi-bilities	Personal growth	Managing people	Crises and fires	Free time	Admin-istrative tasks	Total time/day
Monday	2 hrs	1 hr	3 hrs	0 hrs	0 hrs	2 hrs	8 hrs
Tuesday	3	1	4	0	0	2	10
Wednesday	7	0	0	1	0	2	10
Thursday	0	3	3	0	0	2	8
Friday	1	2	0	1	3	2	9
Total time/ activity	13 hrs	7 hrs	10 hrs	2 hrs	3 hrs	10 hrs	45 hrs
Percentage of time	29%	16%	22%	4%	7%	22%	100%

Source: 20-Minute Manager: Getting Work Done (Harvard Business Review Press, 2014).

CHAPTER 7

A Tool to Help You Reach Your Goals in Four Steps

by Heidi Grant

Creating goals that you will actually accomplish isn't just a matter of defining what needs doing—you also have to spell out the specifics of getting it done. Research shows that you can significantly improve your odds by using what motivational scientists call "if-then planning" to express your intentions. We're neurologically wired to make if-then connections, so they're powerful triggers for action.

Adapted from content posted on hbr.org on October 7, 2015

This tool will help you take advantage of how the brain works. To begin, break down your goals into concrete subgoals and detailed actions for reaching them.

Let's use a hypothetical example to see how this works.

Step 1: Establish your goal.

Goal: Improve team communication.

Step 2: Break down your goal into concrete subgoals.

Subgoal 1: Identify where communication is failing.

Subgoal 2: Create new opportunities for communication between managers and direct reports.

Subgoal 3: Reduce information overload among staff members.

Step 3: Identify detailed actions—and the who, when, and where—for achieving each subgoal.

Action on subgoal 1: Gather feedback on problem areas from employees.

Who-when-where for subgoal 1: Director of HR, at the beginning of the month, email.

Action on subgoal 2: Generate quick weekly status report.

Who-when-where for subgoal 2: All employees, every Friday, to be submitted via email by noon.

Action on subgoal 3: Prohibit knee-jerk forwarding of emails.

Who-when-where for subgoal 3: All employees, whenever emails are forwarded

Step 4: Create if-then plans that trigger actions. Structure your plans as if-then statements ("If *x*, then *y*") using your actions and who, when, wheres from step 3.

If-then plan for subgoal 1: If it's the first of the month, then I (the director of HR) will send out forms via email soliciting suggestions for how to improve communication.

If-then plan for subgoal 2: If it's Friday morning, then I (all employees) will create a summary of progress on current projects and send it (via email) to my supervisor by noon.

If-then plan for subgoal 3: When I (all employees) forward any email, I will include a brief note at the top explaining what it is and why I'm sharing it.

Defining your goal is important. But when you pair that with if-then planning to decide exactly when, where, and how you'll accomplish your goal, you'll pinpoint conditions for success, increase your sense of responsibility, and help close the troublesome gap between knowing and doing.

Heidi Grant, PhD, is Senior Scientist at the Neuroleadership Institute and associate director for the Motivation Science Center at Columbia University. She is the author of the best-selling *Nine Things Successful People Do Differently* (Harvard Business Review Press, 2012). Her latest book is *No One Understands You and What to Do About It* (Harvard Business Review Press, 2015), which has been featured in national and international media. Follow her on Twitter: @heidigrantphd.

CHAPTER 8

Sprints Are the Secret to Getting More Done

by John Zeratsky

Although plenty of experts have proposed systems and philosophies for getting more done at work, my writing partner Jake Knapp decided in 2009 to come up with his own solution: the sprint. This five-day process helps teams focus on one big goal and move from idea to prototype to customer research in that short span of time. The idea is to fast-forward a project, so you can see what the end result might look like and how the market

---

Adapted from content posted on hbr.org on March 15, 2016

will react. It's also a popular construct in agile project management.

At GV, we've tested the process with more than 100 startups, helping them use sprints to answer big questions, test new business ideas, and solve critical challenges. We've seen firsthand, again and again, how they help teams get more done and move faster.

These aren't all-out, late-night, stack-of-pizza-boxes-on-the-conference-table types of affairs that only work for fledgling internet companies though. They work in larger organizations, too, and they fit into a normal working schedule. The sprint day typically lasts from 10 a.m. to 5 p.m., so participants still have plenty of time to see their families and friends, get enough sleep—and, yeah, stay caught up on email.

Why do sprints help teams get more done? They're not just about speed. They're also about momentum, focus, and confidence. The companies who use sprints (in fields like oncology, robotics, coffee, and dozens more) see consistent results from the process. Here are five of the most important outcomes.

Sprints help you start. When a big problem is looming, it can be tough to dig in. Sprints make an excellent commitment device—when you gather a team, clear the calendar, and schedule customer interviews, you commit to making progress. GV portfolio company Savioke found itself in this same situation: The team had spent months developing a delivery robot for hotels, but felt paralyzed by big questions about the robot's personality and behavior. We planned a sprint, and by the end of the week,

Savioke had tested a simple robot personality with actual customers.

Sprints move you from abstract to concrete. Too many projects get stuck in an alternate universe where debates, theories, and hunches are plentiful, but progress is rare. For podcast startup Gimlet Media, an abstract question—"Should we become a technology company?"—was causing anxiety for founders Alex Blumberg and Matt Lieber. They decided to run a sprint on the question and almost immediately had an answer. After sketching out what their potential future as a tech company would look like and floating it with customers, they decided it wasn't necessary to reach their goals as a company.

Sprints keep you focused on what's important. With all the noise, distractions, and demands for your attention at the office, it's almost impossible to see which issues are really the most critical. That's why every sprint starts with an entire day devoted to mapping out the problem at hand. Then, after your team has built a shared understanding of the challenge, you can figure out exactly where to turn your attention. When Flatiron Health started work on a new tool for cancer clinics, it naturally began by focusing on doctors and patients, typical stakeholders for its products. But a sprint helped the team realize that research coordinators (the folks who administered clinical trials) were actually more important. By the end of the week, it had tested a prototype with this group and gotten enough positive feedback to move forward with the project.

Sprints force crisp decision making. Business-as-usual decision making is busted: We strive for consensus; we don't make tough calls; we aren't transparent about how choices are made. The sprint corrects these problems. The leadership at Slack used the process to decide between two fundamentally different marketing approaches. One was unique, bold, difficult to implement, and the CEO's favorite. The other was more conventional but easier to build. The team could have endlessly debated the merits of each approach until everyone agreed on one, or just gone with the CEO's hunch, but instead they launched a sprint to prototype and test both. After a customer test, the results were clear: The simpler marketing was more effective.

Sprints encourage fast follow-up. Your team will accomplish a ton in every sprint, but the knock-on effects—the confidence of knowing you're on the right road—are even more powerful. When LendUp began working on a new credit card for consumers with no or low credit, the team had many ideas for helpful features, but no clue how to prioritize them so it could design and launch the product. In our sprint together, we created fake marketing around all the possible features. Armed with the results—a clear delineation between essential and unimportant—the team went full speed ahead with the card.

Sprints work for teams and organizations of any size, from small startups to *Fortune* 100s to nonprofits. If you're a leader with a big opportunity, problem, or idea, sprints will help you get started, stay focused, decide quickly, and build a workplace where more things get done.

John Zeratsky is a design partner at GV and coauthor of *SPRINT: How to Solve Big Problems and Test New Ideas in Just Five Days.*

CHAPTER 9

Accomplish More by Committing to Less

by Elizabeth Grace Saunders

Believing that more is always more is a dangerous assumption.

There's a cost to complexity. Every time you commit to something new, you not only commit to doing the work itself, but also remembering to do the work, dealing with the administrative overhead, and getting it all done in the time constraints involved.

The unfortunate result of taking on everything that comes your way is that you end up spending more of

---

Adapted from content posted on hbr.org on January 30, 2015

your time managing the work and less time investing in truly immersing yourself in what's most important and satisfying. But the people creating the most value for their organizations take a different approach. They start with having radical clarity on the meaningful work that will create results. Then when something new comes up, they stop and evaluate the new item in terms of what they already know is most important before saying yes. Sizing up new opportunities—from a simple request for a meeting to a large request for a project—isn't about being insubordinate or unhelpful. Instead, it's about recognizing new activities for what they are: a request for time resources that if not managed properly could pose a serious risk to the stellar execution of the most significant priorities.

It's simple math. Each additional project divides your time into smaller and smaller pieces so that you have less of it to devote to anything. Instead, if you reduce the number of your responsibilities, you have more time to devote to each one. On an individual level, you want to strike the ideal balance between the number of projects and the time you need to excel in them. The same principle holds true on department and companywide levels. Promising fewer new projects, new products, and even new customers gives everyone the capacity to deliver breakthrough results on what remains.

The best way to break out of the vicious cycle of overcommitment and underperformance is to very carefully manage what you agree to do. You can actually do more if you take on less. Here are a few steps to take to prevent overloading your plate:

Create a pause. Whenever possible, avoid agreeing to new commitments on the spot. Instead, slow down the decision-making process to give yourself the space to make a reasoned choice. First ask clarifying questions. For example, if someone requests that you take on a presentation, say, "That sounds interesting. What did you have in mind?" Confirm the topic, format, and formality as well, so you can ascertain how much prep work it will require. Then, ask for some time to review your commitments and get back to them with an answer: "I'll need some time to review my current commitments. Would it be reasonable for me to get back to you tomorrow?" People want to be "reasonable," so they'll typically say yes. If this correspondence happens via email, you may not need to ask for the time to come to an answer—just take it.

Say no early and often. If you immediately know that you don't have the capacity to take on a project, say no as soon as possible. The longer you wait, the harder it will be for you to decline the request and the more frustrated the other person will be when they receive your reply. A simple, "This sounds amazing, but unfortunately I'm already at capacity right now," can suffice.

Think through the project. If you want to take on the project, stop to think through what you'd need to do in order to complete it. A presentation might include talking to key stakeholders, doing research, putting together the slide deck, and rehearsing. For a much larger project, the commitment may be more extensive and less clear.

Map out what you know and then make rough estimates of the amount of time you think the steps might take.

Review your calendar. Once you've thought through the commitment, review your calendar to see where you have—or don't have—open space in your schedule (see the sidebar "Don't Waste Those 30-Minute Gaps Between Meetings" for more about taking advantage of free time). In the case of the presentation, if you see that your calendar has open time, then you can commit to the project with confidence and block it out on your schedule. If your calendar has no time free between now and the day of the event, and the presentation would require preparation, you have a few options. The first is to simply decline, based on the fact that you don't have any available time in your schedule to take on anything new. The second option is to consider renegotiating your current commitments so that you could take on the new project. Evaluate the new request with regard to your current projects. Is taking on this new project worth dropping or delaying something else? If you're not sure, ask your manager: "I was asked to do a presentation for XYZ. That would mean that I'll need to take some time away from project ABC. Would you like me to adjust my priorities to accommodate the new request, or would you prefer that I not take on the presentation?" Using one of these strategies allows you to assume a reasonable amount of commitments and stay out of time debt.

Adjust your commitments. If you take on something new that will have an impact on other projects, make people aware of what they can or can't expect from you. They

DON'T WASTE THOSE 30-MINUTE GAPS BETWEEN MEETINGS

by Jordan Cohen

We don't often pay attention to the 30-minute gaps sandwiched between two meetings. For most, they just mean there's some breathing room before the next meeting starts. Time to grab a quick coffee and maybe answer a few emails. On any given day, that might seem harmless, but if you take a long-term view of your month, quarter, or year, these 30-minute spaces can take a real toll on your productivity: four 30-minute gaps in your schedule can add up to 25% of your day. Thinking differently about this floating space pays off. It's there for us if we choose to use it; to write it off as a waste of time is a missed opportunity. Here's how to take back some of your time:

- Take a few minutes at the start of each day to identify the gaps in your schedule.
- Schedule what you want to accomplish in each gap on your calendar. This can be anything from lower-value work that needs to get done (such as expense reports) to larger, finite tasks you've been dreading (such as outlining your next presentation).
- Hold yourself accountable. At the end of the day, look back on your 30-minute tasks and note which ones you've accomplished.

(*continued*)

DON'T WASTE THOSE 30-MINUTE GAPS BETWEEN MEETINGS

These small spaces of time are also good for the kind of work you want to return to and reflect on, like writing an article or pursuing something creative. For instance, I recently started planning for a large project. I used a 30-minute block to start to draft the project charter statement. Later in the week, I revisited the draft. The passage of just a few days helped me gain perspective. When I revisited the charter, I was able to reshape part of the scope.

So stop looking at those 30-minute gaps in your day as a waste of time. They may be the key to turbocharging your productivity.

Jordan Cohen is Head of Organizational Effectiveness, Learning & Development, and Talent at Weight Watchers International. He is an expert on knowledge worker productivity and is a frequent contributor to HBR.

Adapted from content posted on hbr.org on February 11, 2015

may prefer that you not make another initiative a priority, but if you're aligned with your boss and your goals, you're making the right choice. Also, if you let people know what to expect early on, they're less likely to be upset. This gives you the opportunity to work with them on creating a new timeline or on delegating work to someone else with more availability.

Once you're clear on your commitments, get them on the calendar. That way you know you have time and space for the work you've just committed to do. With this honesty in your scheduling, you can do the work and do it well. Give yourself hours at a time or even whole days to immerse yourself in excellence. When you're not trying to eke out 20 or 30 minutes here and there between emails and meetings to move important initiatives forward, you can accomplish work of real value—and enjoy the process.

Elizabeth Grace Saunders is the author of *How to Invest Your Time Like Money* (Harvard Business Review Press, 2015), a time coach, and the founder of Real Life E Time Coaching & Training. Find out more at www.RealLifeE.com.

CHAPTER 10

How to Say No to Taking On More Work

by Rebecca Knight

Sometimes you have too much on your plate or you're just not interested in taking on a project you've been asked to work on. You might not have a choice in the matter, but if you do, how do you turn down the opportunity in a way that won't offend the person who's asked you? How can you avoid being labeled "not a team player" or "difficult to work with"?

Adapted from content posted on hbr.org on December 29, 2015

What the Experts Say

For most of us, saying no doesn't come naturally. You feel lousy disappointing a colleague, guilty about turning down your boss, and anxious denying a client's request. "You don't want to be seen as 'no person,'" says Karen Dillon, author of *HBR Guide to Office Politics*. "You want to be viewed as a 'yes person,' a 'go-to person'—a team player." Trouble is, agreeing to work on too many assignments and pitching in on too many projects leaves you stretched and stressed. Saying no is vital to both your success and the success of your organization, but that doesn't make it any easier to do, says Holly Weeks, the author of *Failure to Communicate*. "People say, 'There is no good way to give bad news.' But there are steps you can take to make the conversation go as well as possible." Here are some pointers.

Assess the Request

Before you respond with a knee-jerk no, Dillon advises assessing the request first by determining how "interesting, engaging, and exciting the opportunity is," and then by figuring out whether it's feasible for you to help. "Think about what's on your plate, whether priorities can be shuffled, or whether a colleague could step in to assist you [on your other projects]," she says. "Don't say no until you're sure you need to." The assessment ought not be a solo endeavor, adds Weeks. She suggests providing the person who's making the request—be it a client, a coworker, or your manager—with "context" about your workload so he can "help you evaluate the scale and scope" of what he's asking. You need to know, for instance, "Is this a small thing that won't take too long? Or is it a longer-term project? And how important is it?" She says the goal is for you to understand "how much your saying no is going to cost the other person" and for your counterpart to grasp the "repercussions of what he's asking."

Be Straightforward

If you realize you have neither the desire nor the bandwidth to help and, therefore, need to turn down the request, be honest and up front about your reasons, advises Weeks. "Too often people start with lightweight reasons and hold back the real reason they're saying no because they think it's too heavy," she says. "But the little, self-deprecating explanations are not persuasive and are easily batted aside. Or they come across as disingenuous." To limit frustration, be candid about why you're saying no. If you're challenged, stay steady, clear, and on message. Dillon recommends describing your workload and the "projects on your plate" by saying something like, "I would be unable to do a good a job on your project and my other work would suffer."

Offer a Lifeline

To maintain a good relationship with the person you're turning down, it's critical to "acknowledge the other side," says Weeks. Be empathetic. Be compassionate. She suggests saying something like: "'I realize that by saying no, this [chore] is going to be put back in your hands.' The other person might not be happy with your answer, but he'll tolerate it." Dillon suggests offering a lifeline by asking if there "are small ways you can be helpful" to the project. Perhaps you can attend brainstorming sessions, read first drafts, or simply serve as a sounding board. Even in saying no, you want to "convey team spirit," she says. If you're unable to offer small favors, be sure to keep workplace optics in mind. "If you're saying you're too busy to help, don't cut out early and don't be seen taking long, chatty breaks at the water cooler."

Don't Be Mean, but Don't Be Too Nice

"The manner in which you say no is so important," says Dillon. "Don't make the other person feel bad for asking you for help." No sighing, no grimacing, no it's-not-my-turn-why-don't-you-ask-Donna? "Be kind, but firm." Watch your tone and your body language, says Weeks. Don't shuffle your feet and "don't use facial expressions to express reluctance or demurral." Strive for a neutral no. It's also vital that you don't leave your counterpart with false hope that your no could eventually turn into yes, she adds. "There is tremendous temptation to soften the no to get a better response," she says. "But when your no is reluctant, flexible, and malleable, it gives the impression of 'maybe I'll change my mind,' and it encourages your counterpart to keep pushing." At the same time, she says, it's reasonable to state that while the answer may be no today, things could change in the future.

Adjust Your Expectations

Even if you follow all these steps, prepare for negative feedback. Your colleague or client "may not be happy; he may punish you or be perfectly content to burn a bridge," says Weeks. "You can influence how the other person reacts, but you can't control it." She suggests "adjusting your expectations" for what you hope to accomplish. You can't please everyone. "Don't look at it as a choice between confrontation and preserving a relationship," she says. Dillon agrees, noting that you shouldn't read too much into the help-seeker's initial reaction. "He feels frustrated. But it may not be personal. Don't assume he's going to be mad at you for three weeks."

Practice

To get better at saying no, Dillon suggests practicing saying it out loud—either alone, behind closed doors, or with a trusted friend or colleague. "Listen to yourself," she says. Your tone should be clear and your demeanor diplomatic. "You want to say no in a way that makes people respect you." Saying no is a skill you can learn, and eventually it'll become easier, adds Weeks. "Think of all the people who have to say no for a living—lawyers, cops, referees, judges," she says. "They do it with dignity. They own what they're saying. And they are accountable for it regardless of strong feelings on both sides."

Case Study: Provide Context About Why You're Saying No

Katherine Hays, the founder and CEO of Vivoom, the Cambridge, Massachusetts, mobile advertising company, says that she must constantly remind herself that "saying no is one of [her] most important responsibilities."

"At a startup, the opportunity is so big and there's so much to accomplish that it's tempting to [take on] everything," she says. "But if you don't have time to do [something] well, you're doing a disservice to the person you said yes to."

A couple of months ago, Katherine had to say no to a potential client—we'll call him Edward—who wanted to use Vivoom's platform for a new advertising campaign. Ordinarily this would have been a prime opportunity. But Edward wanted to launch his campaign in less than a week, and Katherine's team typically needs two to three weeks to get a client up and running on its system.

"I am an entrepreneur, so I am optimistic by nature," she says. "But I had to think long term [about the request]. Sure, there was a shot it could have worked in that time frame, but hope is not a strategy."

When she told Edward no, she first acknowledged that she knew it wasn't what he wanted to hear. She then explained how the Vivoom team operates and provided context about why the process takes multiple weeks. There simply wasn't enough time.

Edward pushed back. He promised to understand if the results of the ad campaign were not as strong as they could be.

But Katherine held her ground. "I told him that I wanted his first campaign on our platform coming out of the gate to be successful, that had I said yes it would have felt good in the short term but not in the long term, [and] that we wanted to work on his next campaign."

This approach helped her win both his trust and his business. His first Vivoom campaign launches early next year.

Case Study: Consider How the Request Works with Your Goals

For Beth Monaghan, the principal and cofounder of InkHouse, a PR firm, saying no used to be a struggle. She'd feel guilty about turning down requests from colleagues and clients, but agreeing to all of them left her feeling stretched and overwhelmed.

Something had to give. A few years ago, she made a list of her top three personal and professional goals for the year. "I carry the list with me wherever I go," she says. "It helps me say no more easily because I see immediately whether or not [the request] fits with my goals. It makes me feel less guilty about saying no and makes me more purposeful about how I choose to spend my time."

Recently, Beth received an email request from a colleague—we'll call her Susan—who runs a business organization with which InkHouse works closely. Susan wrote to ask Beth if her team would be willing to do some in-kind pro bono work for her organization.

Beth was torn. On one hand, Susan's project might be good exposure for InkHouse. On the other hand, Beth had only a certain number of pro bono hours, and she preferred to allocate those to cause-related organizations. (Beth's professional goals include diversifying InkHouse's client base, strengthening its West Coast presence, and "doing good in the world" by donating time and expertise.)

During Beth's assessment phase, she weighed other factors, too—namely, projects to which her team had already committed. "I knew that if we didn't have the resources and ended up doing a bad job on the event, it would burn a bridge and be worse than saying no in the first placc," she says.

Beth decided to decline the opportunity and called Susan to explain why. Her goal was to say no with "clarity, kindness, and respect," she says. "I was really honest about it. I told her my reasons. Her goal was worthy but it just didn't align with mine at this moment—and she understood. But I also told her that even though the answer was no now, things could change in a year."

Rebecca Knight is a freelance journalist in Boston and a lecturer at Wesleyan University. Her work has been published in the *New York Times*, *USA Today*, and the *Financial Times*.

CHAPTER 11

The Most Productive People Know Whom to Ignore

by Ed Batista

A coaching client of mine is managing partner at a very large law firm, and one of the issues we've been working on is how to cope more effectively with the intense demands on his time—clients who expect him to be available, firm partners and other employees who want him to address their concerns and resolve disputes, an inbox overflowing with messages from these same (and still

---

Adapted from content posted on hbr.org on August 20, 2014

other!) people, and an endless to-do list. Compounding this challenge, of course, is the importance of making time for loved ones and friends, exercise, and other personal needs.

When faced with potentially overwhelming demands on our time, we're often advised to "*Prioritize!*" as if that's some sort of spell that will magically solve the problem. But what I've learned in the process of helping people cope with and manage their workflow is that prioritizing accomplishes relatively little, in part because it's so easy to do. Let's define the term: Prioritizing is the process of ranking things—the people who want to take up our time, items on our to-do list, messages in our inbox—in order of importance. While this involves the occasionally difficult judgment call, for the most part it's a straightforward cognitive task. When looking at a meeting request, a to-do list, or an email, we have an intuitive sense of how important it is, and we can readily compare these items and rank-order them.

Here's the problem. After we prioritize, we act as though *everything* merits our time and attention, and we'll get to the less important items "later." But later never really arrives. The list remains without end.

Our time and attention are finite resources, and once we reach a certain level of responsibility in our professional lives, we can never fulfill all the demands we face no matter how long and hard we work. The line of people who want to see us stretches out the door and into the street. Our to-do lists run to the floor. Our inboxes are never empty.

What trips up so many of us is imagining that we can keep lowering that threshold—by working harder, longer, "smarter" (whatever that really means) in the futile hope that eventually, *someday*, we'll get to the bottom of that list.

The key is recognizing that prioritization is necessary but insufficient. The critical next step is *triage*. Medical staff in a crisis must decide who requires immediate assistance, who can wait, who doesn't need help at all, and who's past saving. Triage for the rest of us entails not just focusing on the items that are most important and deferring those that are less important until "later," but actively *ignoring* the vast number of items whose importance falls below a certain threshold. Here's how to triage your work.

Reframe the Issue

Viewing a full inbox, unfinished to-do lists, and a line of disappointed people at the door as a sign of your *failure* is profoundly unhelpful. This perspective may motivate you to work harder in the hopes of someday achieving victory, but this is futile. You will never win these battles, not in any meaningful sense, because at a certain point in your career, the potential demands facing you will *always* outstrip your capacity, no matter how much effort you dedicate to work. You need to reframe the issue. So the inbox, the list, the line at the door are, in fact, signs of success, evidence that people want your time and attention. And ultimate victory lies not in winning tactical battles but in winning the *war*: not an empty inbox, but an inbox emptied of all truly important messages. Not a completed to-do list, but a list with all truly important items scratched off. Not the absence of a line at your door, but a line with no truly important people remaining in it.

Address Your Emotions

Triaging your work is not merely a cognitive process—there's an emotional aspect that needs to be addressed. Actively ignoring things and saying no to people generates a range of emotions that exert a powerful influence on your choices and behavior. This is precisely what makes triage so difficult, and until you acknowledge its emotional dimension, your efforts to control your workflow through primarily intellectual interventions are unlikely to succeed.

This process may well be occurring right now. A moment ago when you read the phrase, "*no truly important people*," you probably flinched a little and thought it was somewhat callous. I flinch when I read it, too, and I wrote it! But this understandable response is exactly why you devote time and attention to people who don't truly merit the investment. There's a fine line between effective triage and being a jerk, and many of us are so worried about crossing that line that we don't even get close.

To triage effectively, you need to enhance your ability to manage these concerns and other, related emotions (and "manage" does not mean "suppress"). As University of Southern California neuroscientist Antonio Damasio has written (and as you've surely experienced firsthand), emotions can undermine effective decision making by "creating an overriding bias against objective facts or even by interfering with support mechanisms of decision making such as working memory."

And this is exactly what happens to you when the active choice to ignore—the decision at the heart of triage—generates emotions that you fail to fully grasp.

When confronted by overwhelming demands on your time, you may feel anxious, scared, resentful, or even angry, but you're often not sufficiently aware of or in touch with these emotions to make effective use of them. They flow through you below the level of active consciousness, inexorably guiding your behavior, but in many cases—and particularly when under stress—you fail to recognize their influence and miss opportunities to make the choices that will best meet your needs.

Improved emotion management is a complex undertaking, but there are a number of steps you can take that help:

- **Change your mindset.** Adjust your mental models to reflect emotions' importance and the role they play in rational thought and decision making. Your beliefs shape your experience.

- **Take better care of yourself physically.** Regular exercise and sufficient sleep demonstrably improve your ability to both perceive and regulate emotion.

- **Engage in some form of mindfulness routine.** Meditation, journaling, and other reflective practices enhance your ability to direct your thoughts, helping you *sense* emotion more acutely, and provide a new perspective on your experiences, helping you *make sense* of those emotions.

- **Expand your emotional vocabulary.** Having a wider range of words to describe what you're feeling not only helps you communicate better with others, it also helps you more accurately understand yourself.

The ultimate goal is to expand your comfort with discomfort—to acknowledge the difficult emotions generated by the need to triage so that you can face your endless to-do list, your overflowing inbox, and the line of people clamoring for your attention and, kindly but firmly, say no.

Ed Batista is an executive coach and Lecturer at the Stanford Graduate School of Business. He is the author of *The Art of Self-Coaching* (Harvard Business Review Press, 2017) and a contributor to the *HBR Guide to Coaching Your Employees*; he writes regularly on issues related to coaching and professional development at edbatista.com. Follow him on Twitter: @edbatista.

CHAPTER 12

Fending Off a Colleague Who Keeps Wasting Your Time

by Dorie Clark

No one intends for their communication to be a burden; it's not like people leave voice mails with the express purpose of distracting you from your most important work. And yet far too often that's the result. You receive their missives with dread because each one entails more time expended and new obligations that you've been dragooned into.

Adapted from content posted on hbr.org on March 28, 2016

It's not malice that leads some people to overtax your inbox or waste your time. Some of your colleagues may simply be less busy—or less efficient—than you are, and their insistence on stopping by your desk to chat or bombarding you with needless information about projects you're working on together can quickly deaden your productivity.

If you have colleagues who are needlessly demanding too much of your time, here are four strategies you can use to deflect—politely—the entreaties of the less productive.

Clarify the Premise of the Request

A colleague sends you a note: Let's have lunch on Thursday; there's a lot to catch up on. How do you respond? If they're a friend and you'd like to see them, fantastic. But before saying yes, especially if you suspect that they have a tendency to treat your time as an infinite resource, it pays to understand what they're really asking. You might assume they want to discuss the status of a project you're collaborating on. But they may have purely social intentions or want to ask your advice about an unrelated matter. You could write back, "I need to confirm some plans on Thursday, so I'll get back to you ASAP. Just so I'm clear, what would you like to talk about?" Their answer will help you make a good decision about whether you'd really like to allocate your time to them, rather than feeling misled afterward if you misread their intentions.

Don't Default to a Phone Call

If you're trying to do important strategic work, even one extra call (or, heaven forbid, a meeting) can have a massively disruptive effect. That's why it's important to politely question the premise (which, for many, is simply a default). When one client booked me for a speaking engagement, she requested a phone call to discuss logistics, even though most details had been previously worked out via email.

Instead, I gently pushed back. I replied to confirm the engagement and added, "My phone schedule in the next couple of weeks is rather tight because I'm in the throes of interviews for my next book . . . Wondering if we could tackle logistics via email instead so I can guarantee a faster response time? Please let me know & thanks." I didn't shut the door entirely on a call, if it were truly important, but forced her to think about the request. She wrote back and said it would be fine to handle the rest via email, saving at least a half hour, and perhaps more.

Strategically Delay Your Responses

Another certain time waster is a rapid back-and-forth of messages. Some people, if they don't have more important priorities, get caught up in the dopamine rush of an email chain. Unless the matter is truly urgent, it can be useful to respond now to clear out your inbox, but use a tool such as Boomerang to schedule it to be sent a few hours, or even days, later, depending on the topic being discussed. The time delay often cools their ardor and allows them to focus on other things in the interim.

Have a Conversation

Having a "meta" conversation with your colleague about the way you work together can be awkward, but if his behavior is persistent, you're going to get annoyed—and your frustration will likely start to seep out in unhelpful, passive-aggressive ways. Instead, bring it up directly and take responsibility for your preferences—and remember, it really is about what helps you work best, rather than him doing something wrong. (Your definition of productivity may not be everyone's.)

You could say something like, "Frank, you've suggested having in-person check-in meetings a few times now, and I wanted to ask you about that. My bias is typically to minimize meetings and try to get as much done on email as possible, but maybe you can tell me a little more about what information you're looking to share. Is there a way we can make it work for both of us?" He may talk about the importance of building a face-to-face relationship—in which case, you might compromise by sharing updates on email, but both attending the monthly office happy hour together, where you can socialize with multiple colleagues at once. Think about how you can respect his desires without simply yielding to his instinctive, time-intensive preferences.

When it comes to promotions, raises, or the success of our entrepreneurial ventures, we're never going to be rewarded for the number of emails processed or phone calls completed. What matters is how well we accomplish the most important tasks, and that can't be done if we're constantly fending off colleagues who don't prioritize time management for themselves—and, consequently, for you. Saving even an hour or two a week to focus on our top goals can make a profound difference in our long-term success.

Dorie Clark is a marketing strategist and professional speaker who teaches at Duke University's Fuqua School of Business. She is the author of *Reinventing You* (Harvard Business Review Press, 2013) and *Stand Out*, and the forthcoming *Entrepreneurial You* (Harvard Business Review Press, 2017). Learn more about her work at www.dorieclark.com.

CHAPTER 13

Give Yourself Permission to Work Fewer Hours

by Elizabeth Grace Saunders

In 2007 I decided enough was enough. I had been running my own business for a couple of years, and I constantly felt stressed. I had no clear boundaries between work and personal time, and I rarely stopped working without feeling guilty. Although I enjoyed my work and was compensated well for it, the constant stress of overwork prevented me from feeling like a real success.

That year was a turning point for me. I made some changes in the way I worked, bringing down my hours from about 60 per week to 50. Over the subsequent

Adapted from content posted on hbr.org on July 13, 2016

years, I gradually reduced my hours to 40 per week. And even though I was working less, I was increasing my revenue.

Through my own experience and in my work coaching clients on time management, I've seen a strong correlation between poor time management, working longer hours, and feeling stressed. It's due to the tension where, intellectually, you desire to work fewer hours but, emotionally, it just doesn't seem appropriate. You feel as if you're already behind, so working fewer hours would only make the situation worse.

You can revise the way you work so that you gradually cut down on your hours. It's not easy at first, and reaching your goal may take a few months. But by managing your time differently, you can work more effectively in less time, discover a renewed passion for your job, and improve your health—especially in terms of sleep and exercise, better relationships, and overall peace of mind. Follow these steps.

What does the end of your workday look like?

Begin by evaluating how you currently decide when to stop working. People often stop when they feel too tired to continue or they observe their colleagues stop. But these signals aren't helpful. Working to exhaustion means you're less productive when you *are* working, and it can also mean you don't have the energy to enjoy your time outside of work. Basing your hours on a colleague's is dangerous because you're putting your time in someone else's hands (someone who may or may not be working effectively).

Establish a weekly hourly goal

Set a target range of hours you want to work in a given time period—for example, 45–50 hours per week—and use that number as a stopping point. If choosing a weekly range is overwhelming, start small by focusing on an incremental goal, like leaving 15 minutes earlier each day. Determine the tasks you need to accomplish on a weekly and daily basis within this schedule to feel comfortable ending your work on time.

Evaluate yourself

Once you're aiming to meet your new target, observe how you work. If you find yourself planning your time but are still working late into the night or on weekends, identify what's hindering you from working your preferred number of hours. Maybe you're in meetings most of the day or get interrupted constantly, so dedicated project work only happens after everyone leaves. Or perhaps a project is understaffed and you're working multiple jobs.

Find the root cause

Identifying the problem allows you to figure out how to overcome it. For example, if you're faced with endless meetings, control the flow by blocking out chunks of time during the week for focused work. For many managers I've coached, this one simple strategy is the difference between working most nights and wrapping up on time. If in-person interruptions cause the largest delay in your work, close your office door during set times of day, work from home one day a week, or (if your company allows it) slightly stagger your hours from the norm so that you're not in the office during peak times. If the interruptions are digital, shut down instant messages and turn off email alerts during part or all of your day so you can focus on important projects instead of being pulled into urgent tasks.

If your overload happens due to the lack of staff on a project, ask for more people or resources. There may not be enough funding for additional head count, but if you ask around, you may discover that a colleague has some excess time or there may be some budget for temporary staff. If that doesn't work, negotiate extensions of your deadlines, table certain projects for now, or delegate projects to someone else.

Be transparent

You might have some awkward moments when someone is surprised that you declined a project or asked to extend a deadline. But being honest with people about what you can or can't get done within the hours you have allows you to work more effectively and enjoy your work in the process.

Front-load your week—and your days

If all this fails and you still can't find enough time, you may need to revisit your planning. Front-load your most important projects. Put in your priorities early in the day or week to make progress on them before the last minute and end work on time without feeling stressed. For example, I plan to complete all of my most important items by Thursday morning so that if anything unexpected comes up (which it usually does), I can wrap up by Friday at 5 p.m. as planned.

Practice self-care

Once you have these practical strategies in place, your emotions are the final element you need to address. You're used to working longer hours, so even when you've completed your most critical items, inevitably you'll think of other things to do. You may feel uncomfortable telling yourself to stop working. When I first decided to limit my hours, I felt as if I was having withdrawal symptoms. My thoughts would return to what needed to be done next, even though I knew it was time to clock out.

Despite this anxiety, I made myself stop. I committed to an exercise class, to meeting with friends, or to taking on a personal project so that I knew I had to leave. After a few weeks of doing this (and discovering that nothing horrible happened), I became less emotionally resistant to the reduced hours. What's more, those personal commitments made me realize what I'd be losing if I kept working beyond those hours.

With the right strategies and commitment, you can reduce your hours and still get your work done—without the stress.

Elizabeth Grace Saunders is the author of *How to Invest Your Time Like Money* (Harvard Business Review Press, 2015), a time coach, and the founder of Real Life E Time Coaching & Training. Find out more at www.RealLifeE.com.

CHAPTER 14

You'll Feel Less Rushed If You Give Time Away

by Cassie Mogilner

The finding: Spending time helping others leaves people feeling as if they have *more* time, not less.

The research: In a battery of studies, the Wharton School's Cassie Mogilner assigned some subjects to help another person—by writing a note to a sick child, for example, or editing a student's essay—and instructed another group of subjects to do something else. In one

---

Reprinted from *Harvard Business Review*, September 2012 (product #F1209D)

study the other group wasted time by counting the letter e's in Latin text, in a second study they did something for themselves, and in a third they simply left the academic lab early. In each experiment the people who lent a hand to others felt as if they had more time than the people who did not.

The challenge: Does giving away your time really make you feel as if you have more of it? Is the secret to productivity being more charitable? **Professor Mogilner, defend your research**.

> **Mogilner:** The results show that giving your time to others can make you feel more "time affluent" and less time-constrained than wasting your time, spending it on yourself, or even getting a windfall of free time. In the first two experiments, my colleagues and I found that people who wrote notes to sick children or devoted a bit of time on a Saturday morning to helping another person were more likely than the other study subjects to say their futures felt "infinite." In the third experiment, people who helped edit the essays of at-risk high school students were less likely to view time as scarce and more likely to say they currently had some to spare. They also acted on those feelings. When we asked subjects who'd assisted the students how much time they could give to doing paid online surveys the following week, they committed to an average of 38 minutes—nine minutes more than the people who had simply been allowed to leave early. The following week, the people who'd edited the essays also ended up actually doing more than

the other group, spending, on average, seven minutes more completing surveys.

HBR: How do you explain this paradox?

My study coauthors—Zoë Chance of the Yale School of Management and Michael Norton of Harvard Business School—and I went in with a few theories. We thought it might be the social connection, the meaning, or the enjoyment associated with helping others that made our study subjects feel more relaxed about their time. But the explanation that emerged in our results is that people who give time feel more capable, confident, and useful. They feel they've accomplished something and, therefore, that they can accomplish more in the future. And this self-efficacy makes them feel that time is more expansive.

To be clear, you're saying people feel as if they have more time. But they don't. In fact, they have less time, since they've given some away. There are still only 24 hours in a day.

Yes, objectively they have less time. But they feel more effective, and that enhances their productivity. Certainly if you're giving so much time away that you're not able to complete other tasks, then it's not going to work. But our research indicates that giving even a small amount of time to someone else should make you feel you can do more in the time you have. In our Saturday experiment, we asked some people to spend 10 minutes helping others and some to spend

30 minutes, and we found that duration didn't make a difference in how much better they felt about the future than the people who had instead spent 10 or 30 minutes on themselves. That's consistent with research on the benefits of money that shows that they have more to do with what the money is spent on than with the amount spent.

Wouldn't time givers feel just as effective if they simply buckled down and did their work?

Perhaps. But we all procrastinate, and we all need breaks, especially when we're stressed. If you use a break to indulge yourself or to do something mindless like watching TV, you might enjoy it, but it soaks up your time perceptually as well as objectively. It won't make you feel less pressured. You're better off picking an activity, like helping others, that makes you feel that you can do more with your day.

Does doing this interview on behalf of a slacker colleague count?

Sure. Anything that entails spending time for the sake of someone else works. It could be for someone you know or for a stranger; volunteering at a soup kitchen or cooking your partner their favorite dinner.

Are there any other techniques readers can try to make themselves feel less time-constrained?

Yes, research shows that thinking about the present moment instead of the future can make you feel less hurried or rushed, because it slows the perceived passage of time. Even just breathing more deeply can work too. In one study subjects who were told to take long, slow breaths for five minutes perceived their day to be longer and felt there was more time available to get things done than those who were told to take short, quick breaths.

Cassie Mogilner is an associate professor of marketing at UCLA's Anderson School of Management. She studies happiness, highlighting the role of time, and she teaches Advertising and Strategic Brand Management to MBAs, for which she received an Excellence in Teaching Award. Her research has been published in *Psychological Science*, *Journal of Consumer Research*, and *Social Psychology and Personality Science*.

SECTION THREE

Find Your Focus

It's easy to succumb to distractions when we have too much to do, especially when the work we have to do is something that feels like drudgery. Or is mindless. Or involves working with a difficult colleague. Any little electronic notification or person walking by your office is a welcome opportunity to do something—anything—else.

But the good news is you can find your focus and zero in on the work that you have to do—even when it's unpleasant. This section of the guide offers tips and tricks for staying focused in the moment—and for strengthening your focus muscle over time.

CHAPTER 15

Five Ways to Minimize Office Distractions

by Joseph Grenny

Bad news for the self-proclaimed multitasker: research continues to debunk the myth that you can productively do more than one task at a time. The human brain simply isn't designed to function this way. Attempting to divide your focus increases stress and decreases performance.

Unfortunately, however, most workplaces are not conducive to focus. They are full of urgent and attractive interruptions that reduce our ability to devote attention in a way that produces both high-quality results and

Adapted from content posted on hbr.org on December 17, 2015

pleasurable engagement. Evidence of our attention's fragility continues to mount. A ringing phone damages productivity, but even a small vibration can impose a substantial cognitive tax. And if that weren't enough, additional studies show just the presence of a phone undermines our focus and weakens interpersonal connections.

Persistent interruptions become especially insidious when we are unaware of the powerful role our surroundings play in shaping our thoughts, moods, and choices. I call this being *environmentally unconscious*. Think of the last time you were reading a book on a flight. As the sun set and the cabin darkened, you began to strain in order to see the words on the page. The gradual change in your environment happened outside your awareness without triggering the obvious fix: turning on the overhead light.

Modern office interruptions seem similarly subliminal. For example, email alert chimes trigger feelings of anxiety and curiosity. In order to relieve the itch, many people disengage from a more important task to check their inbox or phone. While they may not enjoy this disruption, few people pause to consider that they can control it by silencing the phone—or better yet, silencing the phone *and* banishing it to a purse or drawer, out of view.

Simply gritting your teeth and attempting to ignore nagging interruptions doesn't work. Here are five ways to take control of your environment so it stops controlling you.

Monitor emotions

Try this little experiment: The next 10 times you allow yourself to be interrupted, stop and ask, "What was I feeling immediately before I switched tasks?" Most of our interruptions are addictive responses—learned tactics for avoiding uncomfortable emotions.

In a small experiment, I asked college students to journal their interruptions, and I found that over 90% of task switches were a response to feelings of anxiety, boredom, or loneliness. Becoming more aware of the motives behind your response to seductive interruptions will help you develop healthier strategies for managing your feelings—and for resisting that email or phone alert.

Take the easy wins

Unconscious anxiety about incomplete tasks can also make you vulnerable to distraction. Rather than letting worry take control, help yourself focus by simply knocking off a few high-anxiety but low-complexity tasks from your list. Anything on your to-do list that's unfinished draws on your attention. And the interesting thing is that, as David Allen points out in his book *Getting Things Done*, the low-complexity tasks draw disproportionately from that finite reserve of attention.

For example, "Finding a cure for cancer" attracts more of your attention than "Setting a lunch appointment with the boss." However, this latter task tends to draw more than it deserves. So, free up mental energy by simply knocking off any task that takes less than two minutes to finish before focusing on the cure for cancer.

Structure solitude

Carve out time and space for focus. Learn what your most productive times of day are, then schedule blocks of time for concentrated work on complex tasks. And don't just schedule the time: Create a ritual around building a peaceful space. Turn off phones, alerts, and even internet access, if you can. Give yourself a temporal and spatial oasis and then enjoy the space. At first, you may experience withdrawal pains (see "Monitor emotions"). But hang with it.

Build your attention muscle

Attention is a muscle, and the appeal of interruptions is evidence of atrophy or underdevelopment. But the stronger the muscle grows, the longer you can focus on a task. Carl Sandburg shares a relevant story in his book *Abraham Lincoln*. An observer saw Lincoln sitting on a log, lost in thought as he wrestled with an especially vexing issue. Hours later, the observer happened by him again, still in the same position. All at once, a light broke across his face and he returned to his office. Lincoln had the ability to sit with a problem long enough that it surrendered its secrets to him. Be patient as your muscle grows. Time how long you can focus. Allow yourself to gradually increase your sessions of structured solitude to match your ability.

You can also build the muscle by using some of your drive and commute time to simply sit still and allow your mind to sort and present ideas to you. Turn off all media and let your mind relax and follow its own agenda for a fixed period of time. Try five minutes if it's difficult, then increase the time as you discover the creative and therapeutic value of silence.

Take a problem on a walk

If the office environment makes it difficult to exclude interruption, develop a walking plan. Take an interesting and important problem with you on the walk. Moving your body can supplement mental activity. And you'll be less likely to encounter interruptions while in motion.

You don't get to vote on whether our interruption-driven world is influencing you. Instead, you've got two choices: Take control of these distractions or let them control you. If you allow the latter to happen, interruptions will undermine your performance, increase your stress, and weaken your capacity to pay attention.

But it doesn't have to be that way. When you take control of the things that control you, you'll reap the benefits of our always-online world without so many of the costs.

Joseph Grenny is a four-time *New York Times* bestselling author, keynote speaker, and leading social scientist for business performance. His work has been translated into 28 languages, is available in 36 countries, and has generated results for 300 of the *Fortune* 500. He is the cofounder of VitalSmarts, an innovator in corporate training and leadership development.

CHAPTER 16

Train Your Brain to Focus

by Paul Hammerness, MD, and Margaret Moore

Next time you're sitting in a meeting, take a look around. The odds are high that you'll see your colleagues checking screens, texting, and emailing while someone is talking or making a presentation. Many of us are proud of our prowess in multitasking, and wear it like a badge of honor.

Multitasking may help us check off more things on our to-do lists. But it also makes us more prone to making mistakes, more likely to miss important information and cues, and less likely to retain information in our working memories, which impairs problem solving and creativity.

Adapted from content posted on hbr.org on January 18, 2012

Over the past decade, advances in neuroimaging have been revealing more and more about how the brain works. Studies of adults with attention deficit hyperactivity disorder (ADHD) using the latest neuroimaging and cognitive testing are showing us how the brain focuses, what impairs focus—and how easily the brain is distracted (see the work of Makris, Biederman, Monuteaux, and Seidman). This research comes at a time when attention deficits have spread far beyond those with ADHD to the rest of us working in an always-on world. The good news is that the brain can learn to ignore distractions, making you more focused, creative, and productive.

Here are three ways you can start to improve your focus.

Tame Your Frenzy

Frenzy is an emotional state, a feeling of being a little (or a lot) out of control. It is often underpinned by feeling overwhelmed, anxious, angry, and related emotions. Emotions are processed by the amygdala, a small, almond-shaped brain structure. It responds powerfully to negative emotions, which are regarded as signals of threat. Functional brain imaging has shown that activation of the amygdala by negative emotions interferes with the brain's ability to solve problems or do other cognitive work. Positive emotions and thoughts do the opposite—they improve the brain's executive function, and so help open the door to creative and strategic thinking.

What can you do?

Try to improve your balance of positive and negative emotions over the course of a day. Barbara Fredrickson, a noted psychology researcher at the University of North Carolina, Chapel Hill, recommends a 3:1 balance of positive and negative emotions confirmed by research on individual flourishing and successful marriages. (Calculate your "positivity ratio" at www.positivityratio.com.) You can tame negative emotional frenzy by exercising, meditating, and sleeping well. It also helps to notice and name your negative emotional patterns. Perhaps a coworker often annoys you with some minor habit or quirk, which triggers a downward spiral. Appreciate that such automatic responses may be overdone and take a few breaths to notice and name the irritation, which will help the brain let go of the emotion.

What can your team do?

Start meetings on positive topics and with some humor. The positive emotions this generates can improve everyone's brain function, leading to better teamwork and problem solving.

Apply the Brakes

Your brain continuously scans your internal and external environment, even when you're focused on a particular task. Distractions are always lurking: wayward thoughts, emotions, sounds, or interruptions. Fortunately, the brain is designed to instantly stop a random thought, an unnecessary action, and even an instinctive emotion from derailing you and getting you off track.

What can you do?

To prevent distractions from hijacking your focus, use the ABC method as your brain's brake pedal. Become *Aware* of your options: You can stop what you're doing and address the distraction, or you can let it go. *Breathe* deeply and consider your options. Then *Choose* thoughtfully: Stop? or Go?

What can your team do?

Try setting up one-hour distraction-free meetings. Everyone is expected to balance a contribution of thoughtful and creative input with all-in listening to colleagues without distractions (like mind-wandering, laptops, tablets, cell phones, and other gadgets).

Shift Sets

While it's great to be focused, sometimes you need to turn your attention to a new problem. Set-shifting refers to shifting all of your focus to a new task, and not leaving any behind on the last one. Sometimes it's helpful to do this in order to give the brain a break and allow it to take on a new task.

What can you do?

Before you turn your attention to a new task, shift your focus from your mind to your body. Go for a walk, climb stairs, or do some deep breathing or stretches. Even if you aren't aware of it, when you're doing this, your brain continues working on your past tasks. Sometimes new ideas emerge during such physical breaks.

What can your team do?

Schedule a five-minute break for every hour of meeting time, and encourage everyone to do something physical rather than run out to check email. By restoring the brain's executive function, such breaks can lead to more and better ideas when you reconvene.

Organizing your mind, and your team members' minds, will yield a solid payoff. Adding "high-quality focus" is a great place to start.

Paul Hammerness, MD, and **Margaret Moore** are the authors of *Organize Your Life, Organize Your Mind.* Hammerness is an assistant professor of psychiatry at Harvard Medical School. Moore is the founder and CEO of Wellcoaches Corporation, codirector of the Institute of Coaching at McLean Hospital, and teaches the Science of Coaching Psychology at Harvard Extension School.

CHAPTER 17

The Two Things Killing Your Ability to Focus

by William Treseder

I used to wake up, fumble for my phone, and immediately get lost in a stream of pointless notifications. This digital haze continued throughout the day, keeping me from accomplishing important tasks. I was distracted, anxious, and ineffective as a leader. I knew I had to change but could not seem to break free from the behaviors that kept me locked into the same cycle.

My problem is not unique. Many of us stumble through each day in much the same way. Two major challenges are destroying our ability to focus.

Adapted from content posted on hbr.org on August 3, 2016

First, we increasingly are overwhelmed with distractions flying at us from various connected devices. Smartphone and tablet use is spiking, and we now use digital media for an average of over 12 hours per day. This hyperconnected state does not allow us to process, recharge, and refocus.

Second, we rely excessively on meetings as the default form of interaction with other people at work. Studies indicate that we spend anywhere from 35% to 55% of our time, and sometimes much more, in meetings. If we want to stay focused on truly meaningful activity, something has to change.

You and your business will benefit greatly if you can address these issues. You'll enjoy yourself more and accomplish more. The data echoes what our common sense tells us: We need to carve out time for ourselves if we want to remain focused and effective at work. These five daily practices will help.

Practice mindfulness. The single biggest mistake most of us make is in how we start the day. Do you do as I did and immediately roll over and start checking email on your phone? Bad idea, according to Stanford psychologist Emma Seppälä, author of *The Happiness Track*. As she said in an email interview, "By constantly engaging our stress response [when we check our phones], we ironically are impairing the very cognitive abilities—like memory and attention—that we so desperately need."

So what should you do? Try a simple mindfulness practice when you wake up, which can be anything from quietly taking a few deep breaths to meditating for 20 or

30 minutes. Dr. Seppälä explains why this is so important: "Meditation is a way to train your nervous system to calm despite the stress of our daily lives. When you are calmer, you are more emotionally intelligent and make better decisions."

Organize tasks. Another common mistake is letting other people fill in your calendar, particularly in the morning. You have to plan your day to allow enough time to accomplish complex, creative tasks. As entrepreneur, investor, and Y Combinator cofounder Paul Graham described in "Maker's Schedule, Manager's Schedule," his now famous 2009 post, "a single meeting can blow [an entire day] by breaking it into two pieces, each too small to do anything hard in." Creative tasks require dedicated time when you're fresh, not a few distracted minutes squeezed in between meetings. We all love to think we can multitask effectively, but research shows conclusively that we're terrible at it.

Instead of struggling to accomplish what matters, take advantage of your body's natural rhythms. Focus on complex, creative tasks in the morning; these things will tend to be ones you accomplish individually or with two to three other people. Push all other meetings to the afternoon. These simpler, execution-focused meetings with larger groups are easier to handle.

Clean up. Is your desk a mess? What about the desktop of your computer? Your smartphone's home screen? These areas might seem insignificant in the grand scheme of things, but your environment affects your productivity and quality of work in ways we're just starting to understand.

Keeping a clean work environment—both physical and digital—is essential to your ability to stay focused. At work, put everything in a drawer. Create folders on your desktop to get rid of all the random files, and keep only the most important 8–12 apps on your home screen. Turn off all unnecessary notifications. Don't let yourself get distracted by clutter—you'll stay focused for much longer.

Shrink meetings. How many people were in your last meeting? More important, how many of them were actually involved in the creation or fulfillment of deliverables from that meeting? This question might seem like a strange way to stay focused, but countless studies have shown the benefits of smaller teams. Focus and responsibility are more challenging with too many people, which is how you end up with folks staring down silently at their laptops for an entire meeting.

To stay focused, start with your team. Limit the number of people in any meeting to eight or fewer unless the meeting is purely informational. Make sure each meeting results in action items, a timeline for each action item, and one person who is responsible for ensuring that it gets done. That one person is the directly responsible individual, a powerful technique that Apple uses to effectively manage its vast workforce.

Preserve buffers. One reason so many people have a hard time staying focused is a lack of margin. You cannot be on top of your game if you run from meeting to meeting. Switching tasks and contexts is difficult for the human brain at any time, and that ability degrades throughout the day. For busy executives, this means up to 70% of their time at work is wasted.

If you want to avoid wasting time and burning out, add buffer time between each meeting. For every 45–60 minutes you spend in a meeting, make sure to take 15 minutes or more to process, reflect, and prioritize. This will keep you from wasting time. It will also avoid the burned-out feeling that many of us have at the end of each long day. And it should be an easy sell to your colleagues: They'll benefit by adopting this scheduling tactic, too.

Staying focused at work is not easy, but it is doable. These five practical techniques will help you stay on task, accomplish what matters, and enjoy yourself more throughout the day.

William Treseder is a founding partner at BMNT, a problem-solving consultancy in Silicon Valley. He loves to find creative ways to improve the everyday behaviors that define our lives. Trade tips with William on LinkedIn.

CHAPTER 18

Faced with Distraction, We Need Willpower

by John Coleman

Mustering willpower is about more than resisting our bad habits. It's the mental discipline that allows us to cultivate good habits, make better decisions, and control our own behaviors—everything from dieting effectively to powering through difficult problems at work. It's a quality that can separate the most productive business-people from the least productive. And it's a trait that many of us lack. Surveys of more than 1 million people show that self-control is the character trait modern men and women recognize least in themselves.

Adapted from content posted on hbr.org on February 22, 2012

But willpower is an essential quality for personal effectiveness at work, forcing yourself to prioritize the most important items on your to-do list, powering through an endless day of difficult decisions, or simply resisting the urge to eat that extra bag of chips in the office snack room. Want to grow your business or get that promotion at work? Cultivating willpower may be your quickest route to success.

To combat declining willpower, consider a few of the following approaches, based in part on the recommendations of John Tierney and Roy Baumeister, coauthors of *Willpower*:

- **Practice small.** Did you know that by reminding yourself to sit up straight at your desk, you can train the same mental muscle you need to quit smoking or sustainably shed pounds? Research by Roy Baumeister et al. (published in the *Journal of Personality*) has indicated that even reminding yourself to keep good posture on a regular basis can gradually improve your ability to self-regulate, and maintaining a regular exercise routine may improve self-control. Practice small exercises in self-control, and your overall willpower will benefit.

- **Take on your greatest challenges one at a time.** How long was your New Year's resolutions list this year? How many points did you ignore? If you want to shake a particularly trying habit (or build a good one), you should only focus on one major change at a time. Start, for instance, with your resolution to check Facebook or Twitter only twice per day; then, once you're free of that habit, move on to your new diet and exercise plan. In the short term, the amount of willpower you have is fixed, and overloading yourself with new tasks that require it may diminish your ability to accomplish any goal.

- **Monitor, monitor, monitor.** Want to run a fast mile? Time every run. Want to write the next great American novel? Post the word count you've written every day on Facebook for all your friends to see. The more you monitor something (and ask others to help you monitor), the more likely you are to stay on task. Sites like Quantified Self offer an increasingly diverse array of ways to self-monitor, just as sites like Mint.com offer specific opportunities for self-regulation. If you're distracted by social media at work, keep a log of every time you check those sites and force yourself to introduce small goals to reduce the number of times you visit them every day.
- **Find time to replenish.** In the short term, you only have so much willpower, and once it's depleted, your ability to exercise self-control or make sound decisions diminishes dramatically. If you're in a stressful job, for example, your ability to make decisions is worse in the afternoon than in the morning. However, finding downtime and even eating (replenishing your body's glucose) can help you build up your willpower before taking on difficult

decisions or tasks. Skipping or working through lunch may actually have a negative impact on both your ability to make decisions and your ability to work productively in the afternoon.

- **Keep it clean.** A simple way to improve willpower is to operate in a neat environment. Tierney and Baumeister note that environmental cues like messy desks or unmade beds can "infect" the rest of your life and habits with disorder, whereas maintaining a neat and clean environment can help you to maintain order and self-control in the other tasks you confront. If your office or cubicle is a mess at work, make organizing your space your first order of business, and you may find your focus and productivity improving at work.

Willpower is a struggle in the modern era. Our distraction-filled lives make it innately difficult. These are just a few tips to build and maintain willpower, but starting here may help you build a critical personal discipline.

John Coleman is a coauthor of the book *Passion & Purpose: Stories from the Best and Brightest Young Business Leaders* (Harvard Business Review Press, 2011). Follow him on Twitter: @johnwcoleman.

CHAPTER 19

How to Practice Mindfulness Throughout Your Workday

by Rasmus Hougaard and Jacqueline Carter

Many of us operate on autopilot. In fact, research shows that people spend almost 47% of their waking hours thinking about something other than what they're doing.

Add to this that we have entered what many people are calling the "attention economy." In the attention economy, the ability to maintain focus and concentration is every bit as important as technical or management skills. And because leaders need to absorb and

Adapted from content posted on hbr.org on March 4, 2016

synthesize a growing flood of information in order to make good decisions, they're hit particularly hard by this emerging trend.

But you *can* train your brain to focus better by incorporating mindfulness exercises throughout your day. Based on our experience with thousands of leaders in over 250 organizations, here are some guidelines for becoming a more focused and mindful leader.

Wake up right. Researchers have found that we release the most stress hormones within minutes after waking. Why? Because thinking of the day ahead triggers our fight-or-flight instinct and releases cortisol into our blood. Instead, try this: When you wake up, spend two minutes in your bed simply noticing your breath. As thoughts about the day pop into your mind, let them go and return to your breath.

Pause before you begin your workday. When you get to the office, take 10 minutes at your desk or in your car to boost your brain with a short mindfulness practice before you dive into activity. Close your eyes, relax, and sit upright. Place your full focus on your breath. Simply maintain an ongoing flow of attention on the experience of your breathing: inhale, exhale; inhale; exhale. To help your focus stay on your breathing, count silently at each exhalation. Any time you find your mind distracted, simply release the distraction by returning your focus to your breath. Most important, allow yourself to enjoy these minutes. Throughout the rest of the day, other people and competing urgencies will fight for your attention. But for these 10 minutes, your attention is all your own.

Once you finish this practice and get ready to start working, mindfulness can help increase your effectiveness. Two skills define a mindful mind: *focus* and *awareness*. More explicitly, focus is the ability to concentrate on what you're doing in the moment, while awareness is the ability to recognize and release unnecessary distractions as they arise. Understand that mindfulness is not just a sedentary practice; mindfulness is about developing a sharp, clear mind. And mindfulness in action is a great alternative to the illusory practice of multitasking. Mindful working means applying focus and awareness to everything you do from the moment you enter the office. Focus on the task at hand and recognize and release internal and external distractions as they arise. In this way, mindfulness helps increase effectiveness, decrease mistakes, and even enhance creativity.

As your day progresses and your brain starts to tire, mindfulness can help you stay sharp and avoid poor decisions. After lunch, set a timer on your phone to ring every hour. When the timer rings, cease your current activity and do one minute of mindfulness practice. These mindful performance breaks will help keep you from resorting to autopilot and lapsing into action addiction.

Finally, as the day comes to an end and you start your commute home, apply mindfulness. For at least 10 minutes of the commute, turn off your phone, shut off the radio, and simply be. Let go of any thoughts that arise. Attend to your breath. Doing so will allow you to let go of the stresses of the day so you can return home and be fully present with your family.

Mindfulness is not about living life in slow motion. It's about enhancing focus and awareness both in work and in life. It's about stripping away distractions and staying on track with individual, as well as organizational, goals. Take control of your own mindfulness: Test these tips for 14 days and see what they do for you.

Rasmus Hougaard is the founder and managing director of The Potential Project, a leading global provider of corporate-based mindfulness solutions operating in 20 countries. **Jacqueline Carter** is a partner with The Potential Project and has worked with leaders from around the globe, including executives from Sony, American Express, RBC, and KPMG. They are coauthors of the book *One Second Ahead: Enhancing Performance at Work with Mindfulness.*

CHAPTER 20

Coffee Breaks Don't Boost Productivity After All

by Charlotte Fritz

The finding: Taking short breaks during the workday doesn't revitalize you—unless you do something job related and positive, such as praising a colleague or learning something new.

The research: Charlotte Fritz conducted a series of studies on how people unwind from work, looking at everything

---

Reprinted from *Harvard Business Review*, May 2012 (product #F1205D)

from long vacations to short bathroom breaks. In one study she surveyed workers about what kind of "microbreaks" they took during the day and how they felt afterward. Microbreaks unrelated to work—making a personal call, checking Facebook—were not associated with more energy and less fatigue, and sometimes even were associated with increased weariness. Meanwhile, breaks that involved work-related tasks appeared to boost energy (see figure 20-1).

The challenge: Are coffee breaks actually counterproductive? Are we really better off thinking about nothing but work on the job? **Professor Fritz, defend your research.**

> **Fritz:** People definitely believe that "getting away" from work during the day, even for a short time, is helpful. Organizations preach the value of outside walks and encourage employees to use break time to disconnect and recharge. My own research on stress relief indicates there's a value to disconnecting from work. But the findings on microbreaks suggest that during the workday, it may not be the best approach. Nearly across the board, microbreaks that were not job related, such as getting a glass of water, calling a relative, or going to the bathroom, didn't seem to have any significant relationship to people's reported energy (what we called their vitality). Some activities, like listening to music and making weekend plans, seemed to have a negative impact on energy. The only time people showed an increase in vitality was after they took short breaks to do work-related things, such as praise a colleague or write a to-do list.

FIGURE 20-1

People benefit from detaching from work during long breaks, but not during short ones

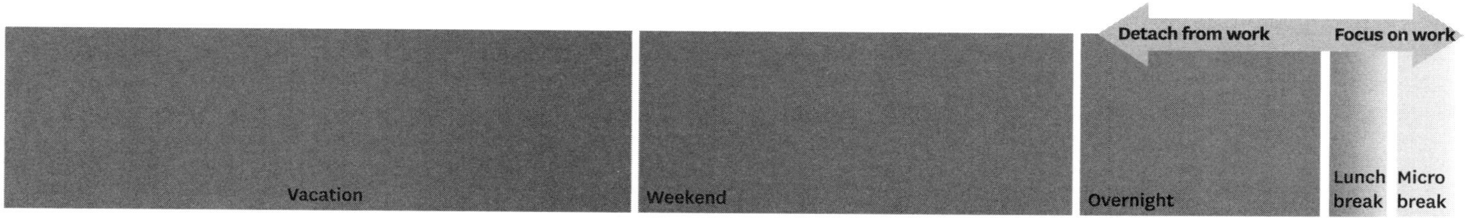

HBR: It just seems implausible that a walk outside during the day wouldn't improve your energy.

Yes, it does seem counterintuitive. Still, going outside for fresh air during microbreaks showed no statistical relationship to vitality and fatigue levels. Helping a coworker did, though. The idea seems to be that when you're in the middle of work, you'll do better and feel better if you focus just on work.

That sound you hear is every manager on the planet forwarding this article to employees with a note that reads, "Get back to work, and you'll be happier!"

Don't misconstrue what I'm saying. It's clear that people need to get away from work in some way or another to recharge their batteries. I started my research looking at vacations. Then weekends. Then time between workdays. Then lunch breaks. Now microbreaks. What we need to do to keep ourselves up and running varies with the time frame, however. This research seems to show that on the job, it's more beneficial to energize yourself through work-related activities.

But intense jobs—stressful negotiations or factory work, say—must require some disconnecting during the day?

Yes—during longer breaks, but not so much during microbreaks. Also, it's important to note that my studies looked just at regular office jobs, some at a software company and a smaller sample at a consulting firm.

A lunch break is good, though, right?

Maybe. We're looking at lunch breaks now, and we've started to see that if people use them to take time to reflect positively on work, to broaden their horizons, to learn something new—which could be job related or not—or to relax, their attentiveness is higher right after lunch and sometimes even still when they leave work. Thus, it seems that work-related and non-work-related activities can be beneficial during lunch breaks.

Couldn't a cup of coffee offer the pick-me-up you need in the afternoon?

No. Coffee breaks were associated with higher fatigue, not lower. That could just be a matter of causality: It might be that being tired makes you drink caffeine, not that drinking caffeine makes you tired. We can't clearly interpret this finding based on the data we have so far. Though I'm not an expert on this, I think some research indicates that caffeine is energizing for a little while, but then you go back to being fatigued and need even more caffeine.

What about vacations? Please tell me they work!

They're good. In most cases they reduce perceptions of burnout and increase perceptions of health. But after about two weeks at work those feelings of well-being drop back to pre-vacation baselines. The length of the vacation doesn't seem to change this effect much, either. But specific positive vacation experiences, like gaining a sense of mastery—climbing a mountain or learning a new hobby—have a positive impact. Part of the quick "fade-out" of the vacation effects may be due to the way your tasks pile up when you're away. So returning from vacation is stressful. This suggests one big vacation a year is not the right model. You'll get the same beneficial effect more often if you take three short vacations.

Your research seems to validate the concept of the 9-to-5 workday, where we come in, work hard, and then leave.

That's the bigger picture. But technology has made it hard to leave work at the end of the day, to achieve what we call psychological detachment. Detachment is well researched and related to all kinds of great outcomes: improved health, sleep, and life satisfaction, and lower burnout. Just one caveat: Too much detachment seems to negatively affect performance. So you can't totally check out. That just means that you don't throw your phone out the window. You just shut it off at night.

I am totally worn out by this interview and still have two hours of work left. I would get a cup of coffee or go to the gym, but you've ruined all that.

Don't be silly. Go praise a colleague, finish your work, and then at the end of the day, go to the gym, detach, and relax.

Charlotte Fritz is an assistant professor in industrial/organizational psychology at Portland State University.

CHAPTER 21

Gazing at Nature Makes You More Productive

An Interview with Kate Lee

by Nicole Torres

The research: University of Melbourne researchers Kate Lee, Kathryn Williams, Leisa Sargent, Nicholas Williams, and Katherine Johnson gave 150 subjects a menial task that involved hitting specific keystrokes when certain numbers flashed on a computer screen. After five minutes the subjects were given a 40-second break, and an image of a rooftop surrounded by tall buildings appeared on their screens. Half the subjects saw a plain

Reprinted from *Harvard Business Review*, September 2015 (product #F1509B)

concrete roof; the others saw a roof covered with a green, flowering meadow. Both groups then resumed the task. After the break, concentration levels fell by 8% among the people who saw the concrete roof, whose performance grew less consistent. But among those who saw the green roof, concentration levels rose by 6% and performance held steady.

The challenge: Can looking at nature—even just a scenic screen saver—really improve your focus? How much can 40 seconds of staring at grass actually help? **Ms. Lee, defend your research.**

Lee: We implicitly sense that nature is good for us, and there has been a lot of research into its extensive social, health, and mental benefits and the mechanisms through which they occur. Our findings suggest that engaging in these green microbreaks—taking time to look at nature through the window, on a walk outside, or even on a screen saver—can be really helpful for improving attention and performance in the workplace.

HBR: How did you measure subjects' performance?

We looked at how many errors people made as well as how quickly they responded to the numbers. This showed us momentary slips in attention—if someone forgot to press a key—and longer dips, when someone drifted off over the course of the test.

People who saw the roof with the grassy, flowering meadow made significantly fewer omission errors, and they had more-consistent levels of attention overall and fewer momentary lapses. But among the group who saw the concrete roof, performance fell after the microbreak.

Did you look at brain scans to measure attention levels?

The behavioral measure we used—the "sustained attention to response task," or SART—had previously been mapped against brain imaging, so we knew that the brain responds in a predictable way when people tap their sustained attention. This is the ability to maintain focus on a task and block out things going on around you. You need to do both to perform well—and to take on tough workloads.

What is it about seeing a green roof that improves our attention? Are we wired to like nature?

In this research, I've been drawing on attention restoration theory, which suggests that natural environments have benefits for people. The theory is that because nature is effortlessly fascinating, it captures your attention without your having to consciously focus on it. It doesn't draw on your attention control, which you use for all these daily tasks that require you to focus. So gazing at natural environments provides you with an opportunity to replenish your stores of attention control. That's really important, because they're a limited resource that we're constantly tapping.

A lot of environmental psychology research has looked only at how people respond to landscapes like forests and woodlands and parks for much longer time periods. We've been wondering if, well, with most of our population now living and working in cities, we should be thinking about smaller green spaces and shorter breaks.

Why 40 seconds? Would 20 seconds work? 5?

There were little clues in the research, where others have talked about how the benefits of nature might be obtained with just brief glimpses through the window—but no one had really explored that idea. So we started to think about the green space you might see in your daily work life. The 40-second time frame came from a pilot study we conducted, in which we had people go through the same procedure, but when they got to the microbreak, they were able to look at the green roof for as long as they wanted before returning to the task. On average, they spent 40 seconds. We don't yet know how brief that break *could* be, but 40 seconds is dramatically shorter than anything studied previously.

Is there extensive literature on microbreaks?

No, there isn't. Some research coming out now looks at opportunities for taking breaks during the day, which is really important. A lot of the literature has looked at longer breaks outside the workplace—at the end of the workday or on weekends or vacations. But now people are starting to think about simple, quick, and effective strategies that are complementary to those other kinds of breaks.

These subjects were just doing simple keystrokes. How would this apply to more-complex tasks?

The task was measuring sustained attention—your ability to maintain focus and not drift off or think about other things. That sounds simple, but it really requires you to lock onto the task. And sustained attention is a fundamental cognitive function that underlies all other networks of attention, like executive attention. It's important for activities like reading, marketing, strategizing, and planning. So our work points to what we might see with more-complex tasks, but we'd need to do more research.

Taking a break to stare out a window could lead to more daydreaming. Is there a point at which this makes us less productive?

At this stage, we just don't know. There are a lot of questions that present opportunities for future research: How do we go about incorporating green microbreaks into our workday? How long do they need to be? How frequently do we need them? How long can the benefits last? These are things we need to be thinking about.

So should I go for a hike in the woods before I start writing?

It couldn't hurt.

Nicole Torres is an associate editor at *Harvard Business Review*.

CHAPTER 22

Five Ways to Work from Home More Effectively

by Carolyn O'Hara

More people are forgoing a lengthy commute and working from home. Whether you're a full-time freelancer or the occasional telecommuter, working outside an office can be a challenge. What are the best ways to set yourself up for success? How do you stay focused and productive? And how do you keep your work life separate from your home life?

Adapted from content posted on hbr.org on October 2, 2014

What the Experts Say

The days when working from home conjured an image of a slacker in pajamas are rapidly disappearing. Technological advances and employers looking to lower costs have resulted in more people working outside an office than ever before. By one estimate, telecommuting increased in the United States by 80% between 2005 and 2012. "The obvious benefits for workers include flexibility, autonomy, and the comfort of working in your own space," says Ned Hallowell, author of *Driven to Distraction at Work: How to Focus and Be More Productive.* And done well, working from home can mean a marked increase in output. A 2013 Stanford University study found that the productivity of employees who worked from home was 13% higher than their office-bound colleagues. People often feel they make more progress when working from home, says Steven Kramer, a psychologist and author of *The Progress Principle,* and "of all the things that can boost people's work life, the single most important is simply making progress on meaningful work." Here's how to work from home effectively.

Maintain a regular schedule

"Without supervision, even the most conscientious of us can slack off," says Hallowell. Setting a schedule not only provides structure to the day, it also helps you stay motivated. Start the day as you would if you worked in an office: Get up early, get dressed, and try to avoid online distractions once you sit down to work. Whether you just started working at home or you've been doing it for months or years, take a few weeks to determine the best rhythm for your day. Then set realistic expectations for what you can accomplish on a daily basis. "Make a schedule and stick to it," says Kramer. Give yourself permission to have downtime as you plan your day. If you have to work extra hours on a project, give yourself some extra free time later on to compensate.

Set clear boundaries

When you work at home, it's easy to let your work life blur into your home life. "Unless you are careful to maintain boundaries, you may start to feel you're always at work and lose a place to come home to," Hallowell says. That's why it's important to keep the two distinct. One way to do that is to set aside a separate space in your home for work. You also want to make sure your friends and loved ones understand that even though you're at home, you're off-limits during your scheduled work hours. "If the doorbell rings, unless I'm really expecting something, I'll ignore it," says Kramer. That not only helps you stay focused, but makes it easier to get out of work mode at the end of the day. "Schedule your time with your family, and with yourself," says Kramer. "Put those on your daily calendar as seriously as you would your work." And don't worry about stopping for the day if you're on a roll with a project. Pausing in the middle of something will make it easier to jump into the task the next day—a tip that is valid for everyone, but especially those working from home. "Ernest Hemingway would try to leave in the middle of a paragraph at the end of the day," says Kramer, "so when he sat down again, getting started wasn't hard because he knew where it was going."

Take regular breaks

It may be tempting to work flat out, especially if you're trying to prove that you're productive at home. But it's vital to "take regular 'brain breaks,'" says Hallowell. How often is best? Researchers at a social media company recently tracked the habits of their most productive employees. They discovered that the best workers typically worked intently for around 52 minutes and then took a 17-minute break. And these restorative breaks needn't take any particular form. "It can be as simple as staring out the window or reading the newspaper," says Hallowell, anything to give your brain an opportunity to briefly recuperate. "The brain is like any other muscle. It needs to rest," says Kramer. "Go for a walk, get some exercise, stretch. Then get back to work."

Stay connected

Prolonged isolation can lead to weakened productivity and motivation. So if you don't have a job that requires face time with others on a daily basis, you need to put in the extra effort to stay connected. Make a point of scheduling regular coffees and meetings with colleagues, clients, and work peers. Get involved with professional organizations. And use online networking sites like LinkedIn to maintain connections with far-flung contacts. Since visibility can be an important factor in who gets promoted (or scapegoated) back at the office, check in as often as you can with colleagues and superiors. "Tell people what you're doing," says Kramer. Share some of the tasks you've accomplished that day. "It's critically important not just for your career, but for your psychological well-being," he says.

Celebrate your wins

When you're working on your own at home, staying motivated can be difficult, especially when distractions—Facebook, that pile of laundry, the closet that needs organizing—abound. One smart way to maintain momentum is to spend a moment or two acknowledging what you have accomplished that day, rather than fixating on what you still need to do. "Take some time at the end of the day to attend to the things that you got done instead of the things you didn't get done," says Kramer. You might also keep a journal in which you reflect on that day's events and note what you checked off your to-do list. The daily reminder of what you were able to finish will help create a virtuous cycle going forward.

Case Study: Stay Organized and Adjust

Freelancing from home for Heather Spohr, a writer and copywriter based in Los Angeles, wasn't her choice. After 10 years in the corporate world, she was laid off from a six-figure sales job, but "I had a baby at home, so I just sort of shifted my focus," Heather says. Today, she writes articles for everyone from parenting and banking sites to "car companies, drug companies, beauty companies, you name it," she says.

Despite wanting to keep regular working hours, Heather often finds that the pressures of finding new writing jobs in addition to executing the ones she's already landed often push her into overtime. "It can be very hard maintaining a schedule because freelancing is so feast or famine," she says.

To give more structure to her working life, she sits down each Sunday evening after her kids have gone to bed and maps out the following week. "I'm huge on lists," she says. "I make daily schedules and prioritize tasks. Then every day I revise that schedule because things come up." She also makes it a habit to include an hour of flex time into her daily schedule. That way, "if my sitter's going to be an hour late, it's not going to wreck my day," she says. "Once I started doing that, my stress level dropped considerably."

She insists on taking regular breaks, setting a timer that goes off every 45 minutes. "Then I give myself 5 to 10 minutes to get up, get a snack, look at Twitter, play Candy Crush, whatever," she says. "At first I felt guilty for doing it, but I would remind myself that when I worked in an office, I'd get interrupted so much more than that. Even with these breaks, I'm still getting more done."

What Heather finds most challenging is the isolation. "I'm very social and extroverted, and I love being surrounded by people," she says. To combat loneliness, she schedules time with fellow writers and friends for face time. She has also found a thriving network of other work-at-home writers in various online discussion groups. "There are lots of people I've clicked with through Citigroup's Women & Co. group and LinkedIn, and there will be chat rooms I'll pop into to say hello and connect," she says.

Case Study: Maintain Work-Life Boundaries

When Catherine Campbell launched her own branding and strategy business in Asheville, North Carolina, in 2014, she already had some experience working from home. Her last job, as marketing director for a copywriting agency, was a virtual one, but she knew that launching her own company would require more discipline. "Managing my time and not overworking was going to be the biggest challenge," she says.

From the start, Catherine set strict rules for keeping her work life distinct from her home life. "It's all about boundaries and mindset," she says. She never uploaded work emails to her phone, so that she wouldn't be tempted to check messages at all hours of the day. She is only available on Skype by appointment and explicitly states in her email signature that her working hours are from 9 a.m. to 5 p.m. EST. "When you leave a traditional office, you're often done for the day," she says. "You have to approach it the same way when maintaining a home office."

She also tries to block out the first hour of each day to check email, do her own promotion and marketing, and make a list of daily goals. "Allowing what I call a quiet hour for myself just to get focused and to knock out some of the smaller tasks allows me to really jump into the larger client work for the rest of the day," she says. She also makes it a point to leave the house every day, rain or shine, at 5 p.m. "I go for a walk, pick up my son, go to a networking group, grab that last item for dinner, or meet with a friend or colleague to talk shop," she says.

She also doesn't sweat the times when she has to work late on a project because she gives that time back to herself later on. "It's what I would call 'smart scheduling,'" Catherine says. "You say to yourself, OK, I have this extra client this week or this project emergency so I'm going to work these two nights. But then I'm going to cut back on Friday and get out of the office at 2 p.m."

"Working from home is always a fine line," she says. "You have to learn how to give and take with yourself so that your business doesn't take over who you are."

Carolyn O'Hara is a writer and editor based in New York City. She's worked at *The Week*, PBS *NewsHour*, and *Foreign Policy*. Follow her on Twitter: @carolynohara1.

CHAPTER 23

Things to Buy, Download, or Do When Working Remotely

by Alexandra Samuel

Whether you're working from home full-time, living life as a road warrior, or simply working the occasional day away from the office, you'll be most effective if you have the right digital infrastructure for remote work. What needs to be in that toolkit depends on the kind of work you do, your personal working style, and your family life: a single software developer may be able to work quietly from her living room with just her laptop, while

---

Adapted from content posted on hbr.org on February 4, 2015

a business development professional with young kids will need a private room with a closed door for remote sales calls.

Whatever the particular circumstances of your remote working arrangements, the following practical tools and practices can make your work at lot easier.

Software

Document collaboration. Google Drive is already the go-to service for sharing documents with colleagues, but it's doubly useful when you're working remotely. Since you can edit a document on screen in real time, collaborating remotely on a draft agenda or report is just as easy as sitting side by side with a paper document—easier, actually, since you'll have all the changes captured by the end of the meeting. You can also use Google Drive or Dropbox to share files and documents that are too large to email.

Note sharing. I use Evernote, a digital notebook application, to keep all my notes and web clippings in one place. It's a terrific tool for remote workers, because it keeps my notes synced across all my devices, so I have access to them no matter which laptop I have with me, and if I only have my phone or iPad. Using Evernote is just like handing off a physical file to a colleague: By inviting someone into a shared notebook, I can easily share work in progress.

Calendaring. If you need to schedule more than the occasional meeting or phone call, set up your calendar with appointment slots that let other people book themselves into your schedule. You can use Google Calendar's appointment slots, or use a service like Calendly. Establish appointment windows during a specific chunk of the day or week, and keep your prime concentration hours (whenever they are) blocked off to do the kind of uninterrupted work that's hard to do in the office.

Screen sharing. Even if you aren't doing sales calls, screen sharing is often the most efficient way to show someone what you're talking about. I find join.me is the most reliable option, and the basic version is free. If you *are* doing sales calls or demos, set up accounts on a couple of different providers so that you have a fallback if your usual service doesn't work for whomever you're trying to share with.

Instant messaging. Instant messaging provides many of the benefits of collegiality, without the disruption of a ringing phone or a colleague plopping themselves down at your desk when you're working toward a key deadline. Use it to ask someone a quick question, or even for a little bit of lightweight socializing that can cut down on the isolation of remote work. It's most effective if you use the same chat service as the lion's share of your colleagues or clients, and if you hook it up to your phone's SMS account so that you can read and respond to text messages on your laptop.

Social networking. Even if you've never been a fan of Facebook or Twitter, remote work is a great reason to embrace one or more social networks. It's a way to get some of the ambient sociability and serendipity of working in an office: A five-minute Twitter break can give you a sounding board for a new idea, or let you discover that bit of industry news you'd otherwise miss. Choose one social network that will be your virtual watercooler, and drop in at least a couple of times a day so that you're not cut off from the world.

Hardware

All those great cloud-based collaboration tools won't do you any good if you can't get online . . . or turn on your computer. Here's what I recommend keeping on hand so you've always got the access you need.

Your own hot spot. You can't depend on the vagaries of coffee shop Wi-Fi, so produce your own internet connection anywhere, anytime. That could be as simple as tethering to your phone and using it as your backup connection, or buying a USB stick from your wireless company so you can access cell data from your laptop.

A great headset. Get a reliable headset for both your home and mobile phone. I've tried a dozen different Bluetooth headsets and headphones, but I prefer using a wired headset so I don't have to worry about charging and pairing. Using a headset lets you type while you talk, but one of the benefits of remote work is that you don't *have* to sit at your desk. If you've got a call that doesn't require note taking, your headset lets you go for an energizing walk or gives you the time to clean up your desk (or your kitchen).

A mini travel charger. If you carry your own power strip, you'll never find yourself in a café where all the power outlets are already spoken for: Just ask someone if you can unplug their computer so you can *both* use your power strip. This trick will help you make friends in crowded convention centers or airport lounges, too.

Extra cables. Buy an extra charging adapter for your computer and extras cables for all your devices (phone, tablet, and so on). If you keep all your cables in your bag, rather than unplugging them at home every morning, you'll never find yourself stuck with a dead device and a missing charger.

Battery and car adapter. Carry an external battery that can charge your phone and that you can also charge in the car. Better yet, buy an inverter that will allow you to plug your laptop into your car, so you can always take that crucial sales call from the privacy of your vehicle, without worrying that you'll lose power mid-presentation.

A lightweight laptop. The more mobile you are, the easier it is to work anywhere, anytime.

Best Practices

Even the best work-from-home toolkit can't guarantee that you'll be happy and productive as a remote worker. To make your remote work setup *really* effective, take advantage of the number-one benefit of remote work: the opportunity to exercise a high degree of intention and control over what you want your workday to look like. Here are my top three recommendations.

Chunk your day. Break your day into sections that focus your attention on what kinds of work you want to do when. For me, that means dividing my workday into "open door" and "closed door" periods. I work best first thing in the morning, so I try to keep my morning schedule blocked off for focused work.

Keep an emergency channel. One of the great things about working remotely is that you're not subject to constant interruption from colleagues. To take advantage of that, I leave my phone on silent and my instant messaging status as "unavailable." But my closest colleagues know that they can always reach me via SMS.

Plan for connection. Staying connected to other people is just as important as protecting concentrated work time. Working at coffee shops is a great way to avoid becoming a hermit, especially if you choose a regular spot and introduce yourself to the baristas. Schedule lunches or drinks with colleagues and friends so that you don't get too isolated: Remember that you're getting a *lot* more work done when you're out of the office, so you can afford a little social time.

One of the great benefits of living in an online world is the ability to work anywhere and anytime. Harness that power and tailor your setup to work where and how you work, and you'll be more productive than any 9-to-5 clock puncher.

Alexandra Samuel is a speaker, researcher, and writer who works with the world's leading companies to understand their online customers and craft data-driven reports like "Sharing Is the New Buying." The author of *Work Smarter with Social Media* (Harvard Business Review Press, 2015), Alex holds a PhD in political science from Harvard University. Follow her on Twitter: @awsamuel.

SECTION FOUR

Motivate Yourself

You've set goals for yourself and planned your day. You've said no to some projects and yes to others, and drawn boundaries with demanding colleagues.

Now that you've found your focus and are digging into your work, how can you keep that momentum going? This section of the guide will help you keep chipping away at the task at hand.

CHAPTER 24

Finding Meaning at Work, Even When Your Job Is Dull

by Morten Hansen and Dacher Keltner

Do you experience meaning at work—or just emptiness?

In the United States, people spend on average 35–40 hours working every week. That's some 80,000 hours during a career—more time than you will probably spend with your kids. Beyond the paycheck, what does work give you? Few questions could be more important. It's sad to walk through life and experience work as an empty, dreadful chore—sapping energy out of your body

---

Adapted from content posted on hbr.org on December 20, 2012

and soul. Yet many employees do, as evidenced by one large-scale study showing that only 31% of employees were engaged.

Work can, however, provide an array of meaningful experiences, even though many employees don't enjoy those in their current job. So, what *are* the sources of meaningful experiences at work?

We've compiled a list based on our reading of literature in organization behavior and psychology. Many theories speak to meaning at work, including need-based, motivational, status, power, and community theories. The phrase "meaning at work" refers to a person's experience of something meaningful—something of value—that work provides. That is not the same as "meaningful work," which refers to the task itself. Work is a social arena that provides other kinds of meaningful experiences as well.

Before we run through the list, it's important to note that different people look for different types of meaning at work and that different workplaces provide different meanings.

If your job has any of the following aspects, then it's likely that you experience meaning at work, which can be more motivational than any salary bump or success on an individual project.

Purpose

Contributions beyond yourself

The people at Kiva, a nonprofit, channel microloans to poor people who can use the money to start a small business and improve their lives. Their work clearly has a greater purpose—that of helping people in need. This taps into a longing to have a meaningful life defined as making contributions beyond oneself.

The problem is, however, that most work doesn't have such a higher purpose, either because work is basically mundane or because—let's face it—the company doesn't really have a social mission. Critics like Umair Haque argue that work that involves selling yet more burgers, sugar water, high-fashion clothes, and the like has no broader purpose whatsoever. In this view, Coke's "Open Happiness" is just a slogan devoid of meaning. However, as Teresa Amabile and Steve Kramer argue, much work can be infused with some level of purpose. Companies that make real efforts in social responsibilities do this; for example, Danone, the $25 billion, highly successful consumer goods company selling yogurt, has defined its business as providing healthy foods (which led it to sell off its biscuit business). The litmus test here is whether employees *experience* that their work makes positive contributions to others. Then they experience meaning at work.

Self-Realization

Learning

Many MBA graduates flock to McKinsey, BCG, and other consultancies so that they can rapidly acquire valuable skills. General Electric is renowned for developing general managers; and people who want to become marketers crave to learn that trade at Procter & Gamble. Work offers personal growth: opportunities to learn, expand horizons, and improve self-awareness.

Accomplishment

Work is a place to accomplish things and be recognized, which leads to greater satisfaction, confidence, and self-worth. In the documentary *Jiro Dreams of Sushi*, we see Japan's greatest sushi chef devote his life to making perfect sushi. Well, some critics like Lucy Kellaway at the *Financial Times* say there isn't a real social mission here. But, from watching the movie, his quest for perfection—to make better sushi, all the time—gives his life a deep sense of meaning. And for Jiro, the work itself—making the sushi—gives him a deep intrinsic satisfaction.

Prestige

Status

At cocktail parties, a frequent question is, "Where do you work?" The ability to rattle off a name like, "Oh, I'm a doctor at Harvard Medical School" oozes status. For some, that moment is worth all the grueling nightshifts. A high-status organization confers respect, recognition, and a sense of worth on employees, and that provides meaning at work for some.

Power

Paul Lawrence and Nitin Nohria wrote in their book *Driven*, that, for those drawn to power, work provides an arena for acquiring and exercising power. You may not be one of those, but if you are, you experience work as meaningful because you have and can use power.

Social

Belonging to a community

Companies like Southwest Airlines go out of their way to create a company atmosphere where people feel they belong. In a society where they increasingly are bowling alone, people crave a place where they can forge friendships and experience a sense of community. The workplace can complement or even be a substitute for other communities (family, the neighborhood, clubs, and so on).

Agency

Employees experience meaning at work when what they do actually matters for the organization—when their ideas are listened to and when they see that their contributions have an impact on how the place performs.

Autonomy

As Dan Pink shows in his book *Drive*, autonomy is a great intrinsic motivator. Some people are drawn to certain kinds of work that provide a great deal of autonomy—the absence of others who tell you what to do, and the freedom to do your own work and master your task. For example, entrepreneurs frequently go into business by themselves so that they can be their own boss.

There are no doubt other sources as well, but these aspects seem to be especially important. Encountering several of these elements at work is not necessarily better. Experiencing one deeply may just be enough. But chances are that if you don't experience any of these, you probably have a hard time going to work every day.

Morten Hansen is a professor at the University of California, Berkeley, and at INSEAD, France, as well as author of *Collaboration* (Harvard Business Review Press, 2009). **Dacher Keltner** is a professor of psychology at UC Berkeley and the author of *Born to Be Good: The Science of a Meaningful Life*.

CHAPTER 25

How to Make Yourself Work When You Just Don't Want To

by Heidi Grant

There's that project you've left on the back burner—the one with the deadline that's growing uncomfortably near. And there's the client whose phone call you really should return—the one who does nothing but complain and eat up your valuable time. Wait, weren't you going to try to go to the gym more often this year?

Adapted from content posted on hbr.org on February 14, 2014

Can you imagine how much less guilt, stress, and frustration you would feel if you could somehow just make yourself do the things you don't want to do when you are actually supposed to do them? Not to mention how much happier and more effective you would be?

The good news (and it's very good news) is that you can get better about not putting things off, if you use the right strategy. Figuring out which strategy to use depends on why you're procrastinating in the first place. Let's take a look at the most common reasons for procrastination.

Reason 1: You're putting something off because you're afraid you'll screw it up

Solution: Adopt a "prevention focus"

There are two ways to look at any task. You can do something because you see it as a way to *end up better off than you are now*—as an achievement or accomplishment. As in, *if I complete this project successfully, I will impress my boss*, or *if I work out regularly, I will look amazing*. Psychologists call this a **promotion focus**, and research shows that when you have one, you're motivated by the thought of making gains and work best when you feel eager and optimistic. Sounds good, doesn't it? Well, if you're afraid you'll screw up on the task in question, this is *not* the focus for you. Anxiety and doubt undermine promotion motivation, leaving you less likely to take any action at all.

What you need is a way of looking at what you have to do that isn't undermined by doubt—ideally, one that thrives on it. When you have a **prevention focus**, instead of thinking about how you can end up better off, you see the task as a way to *hang on to what you've already got*—to avoid loss. For the prevention focused, successfully completing a project is a way to keep your boss from being angry or thinking less of you. Working out regularly is a way to not "let yourself go." Decades of research, which I describe in my book *Focus*, shows that prevention motivation is actually enhanced by anxiety about what might go wrong. When you're focused on avoiding loss, it becomes clear that the only way to get out of danger is to take immediate action. The more worried you are, the faster you are out of the gate.

I know this doesn't sound like a barrel of laughs, particularly if you're usually more the promotion-minded type, but there is probably no better way to get over your anxiety about screwing up than to give some serious thought to all the dire consequences of doing nothing at all. Go on, scare the pants off yourself. It feels awful, but it works.

Reason 2: You're putting something off because you don't "feel" like doing it

Solution: Make like Spock and ignore your feelings. They're getting in your way

In his excellent book *The Antidote: Happiness for People Who Can't Stand Positive Thinking*, Oliver Burkeman points out that much of the time, when we say things like "I just can't get out of bed early in the morning," or "I just can't get myself to exercise," what we really mean is that we can't get ourselves to feel like doing these things. After all, no one is tying you to your bed every morning. Intimidating bouncers aren't blocking the entrance to your gym. Physically, nothing is stopping you—you just don't feel like it. But as Burkeman asks, "Who says you need to wait until you 'feel like' doing something in order to start doing it?"

Think about that for a minute, because it's really important. Somewhere along the way, we've all bought into the idea—without consciously realizing it—that to be motivated and effective we need to *feel* like we want to take action. We need to be eager to do so. I really don't know why we believe this, because it's 100% nonsense. Yes, on some level you need to be committed to what you're doing; you need to want to see the project finished, or get healthier, or get an earlier start to your day. But you don't need to *feel like doing it.*

In fact, as Burkeman points out, many of the most prolific artists, writers, and innovators have become so in part because of their reliance on work routines that forced them to put in a certain number of hours a day, no matter how uninspired (or, in many instances, hung over) they might have felt. Burkeman reminds us of renowned artist Chuck Close's observation that "inspiration is for amateurs. The rest of us just show up and get to work."

So if you're sitting there, putting something off because you don't feel like doing it, remember that you don't actually need to feel like doing it. *There is nothing stopping you.*

Reason 3: You're putting something off because it's hard, boring, or otherwise unpleasant

Solution: Use if-then planning

Too often, we try to solve this particular problem with sheer will: *Next time, I will* ***make*** *myself start working on this sooner.* Of course, if we actually *had* the willpower to do that, we would never put it off in the first place (see chapter 18, "Faced with Distraction, We Need Willpower"). Studies show that people routinely overestimate their capacity for self-control and rely on it too often to keep them out of hot water.

Do yourself a favor, and embrace the fact that your willpower is limited, and that it may not always be up to the challenge of getting you to do things you find difficult, tedious, or otherwise awful. Instead, use **if-then planning** to get the job done.

Making an *if-then* plan is more than just deciding what specific steps you need to take to complete a project; it's also deciding *where* and *when* you will take them.

> **If** it is 2 p.m., **then** I will stop what I'm doing and start work on the report Bob asked for.

> **If** my boss doesn't mention my request for a raise at our meeting, **then** I will bring it up again before the meeting ends.

By deciding in advance *exactly* what you're going to do, and when and where you're going to do it, there's no deliberating when the time comes. No *do I really have to do this now?*, or *can this wait till later?*, or *maybe I should do something else instead.* It's when we deliberate that willpower becomes necessary to make the tough choice. But if-then plans dramatically reduce the demands placed on your willpower by ensuring that you've made the *right* decision way ahead of the critical moment. In fact, if-then planning has been shown in over 200 studies to increase rates of goal attainment and productivity by 200% to 300%, on average.

I realize that the three strategies I'm offering you—thinking about the consequences of failure, ignoring your feelings, and engaging in detailed planning—don't sound like as much fun as advice like "Follow your passion!" or "Stay positive!" But they have the decided advantage of actually being *effective*, which, as it happens, is exactly what you'll be if you use them.

Heidi Grant, PhD is Senior Scientist at the Neuroleadership Institute and associate director for the Motivation Science Center at Columbia University. She is the author of the best-selling *Nine Things Successful People Do Differently* (Harvard Business Review Press, 2012). Her latest book is *No One Understands You and What to Do About It* (Harvard Business Review Press, 2015), which has been featured in national and international media. Follow her on Twitter: @heidigrantphd.

CHAPTER 26

How to Beat Procrastination

by Caroline Webb

Procrastination comes in many disguises. We might resolve to tackle a task, but find endless reasons to defer it. We might prioritize things we can readily tick off our to-do list—answering emails, say—while leaving the big, complex stuff untouched for another day. We can look and feel busy, while artfully avoiding the tasks that really matter. And when we look at those rolling, long-untouched items at the bottom of our to-do list, we can't help but feel a little disappointed in ourselves.

The problem is our brains are programmed to procrastinate. In general, we all tend to struggle with tasks

Adapted from content posted on hbr.org on July 29, 2016

that promise *future* upside in return for efforts we take *now*. That's because it's easier for our brains to process concrete rather than abstract things, and the immediate hassle is very tangible compared with those unknowable, uncertain future benefits. So the short-term effort easily dominates the long-term upside in our minds—an example of something that behavioral scientists call *present bias*.

How can you become less myopic about your elusive tasks? It's all about rebalancing the cost-benefit analysis: Make the benefits of action feel bigger and the costs of action feel smaller. The reward for doing a pestering task needs to feel larger than the immediate pain of tackling it.

Make the Benefits of Action Feel Bigger and More Real

Visualize how great it will be to get it done

Researchers have discovered that people are more likely to save for their future retirement if they're shown digitally aged photographs of themselves. Why? Because it makes their future selves feel more real, making the future benefits of saving also feel weightier. When you apply a lo-fi version of this technique to any task you've been avoiding, by taking a moment to paint yourself a vivid mental picture of the benefits of getting it done, it can sometimes be just enough to get you unstuck. So if there's a call you're avoiding or an email you're putting off, give your brain a helping hand by imagining the virtuous sense of satisfaction you'll have once it's done—

and perhaps also the look of relief on someone's face as they get from you what they needed.

Precommit, publicly

Telling people that we're going to get something done can amplify the appeal of actually taking action, because our brain's reward system is so responsive to our social standing. Research has found that it matters greatly to us whether we're respected by others—even by strangers. Most of us don't want to look foolish or lazy to other people. So by daring to say "I'll send you the report by the end of the day," you add social benefits to following through on your promise, which can be just enough to nudge you to bite the bullet.

Confront the downside of inaction

We're strangely averse to properly evaluating the status quo, research has found. While we might weigh the pros and cons of doing something new, we far less often consider the pros and cons of *not* doing that thing. Known as *omission bias*, this often leads us to ignore some obvious benefits of getting stuff done. Suppose you're repeatedly putting off the preparation you need to do for an upcoming meeting. You're tempted by more exciting tasks, so you tell yourself you can do it tomorrow (or the day after). But force yourself to think about the downside of putting it off, and you realize that tomorrow will be too late to get the input you really need from colleagues. If you get moving *now*, you have half a chance of reaching them in time, so finally, your gears creak into action.

Make the Costs of Action Feel Smaller

Identify the first step

Sometimes we're just daunted by the task we're avoiding. We might have "learn French" on our to-do list, but who can slot that into the average afternoon? The trick here is to break down big, amorphous tasks into baby steps that don't feel as effortful. Even better: Identify the very *smallest* first step, something that's so easy that even your present-biased brain can see that the benefits outweigh the costs of effort. So instead of "learn French," you might decide to "email Nicole to ask advice on learning French." Achieve that small goal, and you'll feel more motivated to take the next small step than if you'd continued to beat yourself up about your lack of language skills.

Tie the first step to a treat

We can make the cost of effort feel even smaller if we link that small step to something we're actually looking forward to doing. In other words, tie the task that you're avoiding to something that you're *not* avoiding. For example, you might allow yourself to read lowbrow magazines or books when you're at the gym, because the guilty pleasure helps dilute your brain's perception of the short-term "cost" of exercising. Likewise, you might muster the self-discipline to complete a slippery task if you promise yourself you'll do it in a nice café with a favorite drink in hand.

Remove the hidden blockage

Sometimes we find ourselves returning to a task repeatedly, still unwilling to take the first step. We hear a little voice in our head saying, "Yeah, good idea, but . . . no." At this point, we need to ask that voice some questions, to figure out what's really making it unappealing to take action. This doesn't necessarily require psychotherapy. Patiently ask yourself a few "why" questions—"why does it feel tough to do this?" and "why's that?"—and the blockage can surface quite quickly. Often, the issue is that a perfectly noble, competing commitment is undermining your motivation. For example, suppose you were finding it hard to stick to an early-morning goal-setting routine. A few "whys" might highlight that the challenge stems from your equally strong desire to eat breakfast with your family. Once you've made that conflict more explicit, you're more likely to find a way to overcome it—perhaps by setting your daily goals the night before, or on your commute into work.

So the next time you find yourself mystified by your inability to get important tasks done, be kind to yourself. Recognize that your brain needs help if it's going to be less shortsighted. Try taking at least one step to make the benefits of action loom larger and one to make the costs of action feel smaller. Your languishing to-do list will thank you.

Caroline Webb is the author of *How to Have a Good Day: Harness the Power of Behavioral Science to Transform Your Working Life*. She is also CEO of coaching firm Sevenshift, and Senior Adviser to McKinsey & Company. Follow her on Facebook, Google+, or on Twitter: @caroline_webb_.

CHAPTER 27

Steps to Take When You're Starting to Feel Burned Out

by Monique Valcour

Burnout hurts. When you burn out at work, you feel diminished, like a part of yourself has gone into hiding. Challenges that were formerly manageable feel insurmountable. It's the opposite end of the spectrum from engagement. The engaged employee is energized, involved, and high performing; the burned-out employee is exhausted, cynical, and overwhelmed.

Adapted from content posted on hbr.org on June 20, 2016

Research shows that burnout has three dimensions: emotional exhaustion, depersonalization, and reduced personal accomplishment. When you're emotionally exhausted, you feel used up—not just emotionally, but often physically and cognitively as well. You can't concentrate. You're easily upset or angered, you get sick more often, and you have difficulty sleeping. Depersonalization shows up in feelings of alienation from and cynicism toward the people your job requires you to interact with. One of my coaching clients summed it up like this: "I feel like I'm watching myself in a play. I know my role, I can recite my lines, but I just don't care." What's worse, although you can't imagine going on like this much longer, you don't see a feasible way out of your predicament.

This third dimension of burnout—reduced personal accomplishment—traps many employees in situations where they suffer. When you're burned out, your capacity to perform is compromised, and so is your belief in yourself. In an insidious twist, employers may misinterpret an employee suffering from burnout as an uncooperative low performer rather than as a person in crisis. When that's the case, you're unlikely to get the support you desperately need.

Burnout occurs when the demands people face on the job outstrip the resources they have to meet them, research shows. Certain types of demands are much more likely to tax people to the point of burnout, especially a heavy workload, intense pressure, and unclear or conflicting expectations. A toxic interpersonal environment—whether it shows up as undermining, backstabbing, incivility, or low trust—is a breeding ground for burnout because it requires so much emotional effort just to cope with the situation. Role conflict, which occurs when the expectations of one role that's important to you conflict with those of another, also increases risk of burnout. This might happen, for example, when the demands of your job make it impossible to spend adequate time with your loved ones, or when the way you're expected to act at work clashes with your sense of self.

If you think you might be experiencing burnout, don't ignore it; it won't go away by itself. The consequences of burnout for individuals are grave, including coronary disease, hypertension, gastrointestinal problems, depression, anxiety, increased alcohol and drug use, marital and family conflict, alienation, sense of futility, and diminished career prospects. The costs to employers include decreased performance, absenteeism, turnover, increased accident risk, lowered morale and commitment, cynicism, and reduced willingness to help others.

To get back to thriving, it's essential to understand that burnout is fundamentally a state of resource depletion. In the same way that you can't continue to drive a car that's out of fuel just because you'd like to get home, you can't overcome burnout simply by deciding to "pull yourself together." Rebounding from burnout and preventing its recurrence requires three things: replenishing lost resources, avoiding further resource depletion, and finding or creating resource-rich conditions going forward. Many resources are vital for our performance and well-being, from personal qualities like skills, emotional stability, and good health, to supportive relationships with colleagues, autonomy and control at work, constructive feedback, having a say in matters that affect us, and feeling that our work makes a difference. Try the following steps to combat burnout.

Prioritize taking care of yourself to replenish personal resources. Start by making an appointment with your doctor and getting an objective medical assessment. I encourage clients to take a lesson from the safety briefing provided at the beginning of every commercial flight, which instructs passengers to "secure your own oxygen mask before helping others." If you want to be able to perform, you need to shore up your capacity to do so. Prioritize good sleep habits, nutrition, exercise, connection with people you enjoy, and practices that promote calmness and well-being, like meditation, journaling, talk therapy, or simply quiet time alone doing an activity you enjoy.

Analyze your current situation. Perhaps you already understand what's burning you out. If not, try this: track how you spend your time for a week (either do this on paper, in a spreadsheet, or in one of the many apps now available for time tracking). For each block of time, record what you're doing, whom you're with, how you feel (for example, on a scale of 1 to 10 where 0 = angry or depressed and 10 = joyful or energized), and how valuable the activity is. This gives you a basis for deciding where to make changes that will have the greatest impact. Imagine that you have a fuel gauge you can check to see the level of your personal resources (physical, mental, and emotional) at any moment. The basic principle is to limit your exposure to the tasks, people, and situations that drain you and increase your exposure to those that replenish you.

Reduce exposure to job stressors. Your condition may warrant a reduction in your workload or working hours, or taking some time away from work. Using your analysis of time spent and associated mood or energy level and value of activity as a guide, jettison low value–high frustration activities to the extent possible. If you find that there are certain relationships that are especially draining, limit your exposure to those people. Reflect on whether you have perfectionist tendencies; if so, consciously releasing them will lower your stress level. Delegate the things that aren't necessary for you to do personally. Commit to disconnecting from work at night and on the weekends.

Increase job resources. Prioritize spending time on the activities that are highest in value and most energizing. Reach out to people you trust and enjoy at work. Look for ways to interact more with people you find stimulating. Talk to your boss about what resources you need to perform at your peak. For instance, if you lack certain skills, request training and support for increased performance, such as regular feedback and mentoring by someone who's skilled. Brainstorm with colleagues about ways to modify work processes to make everyone more resourceful. For instance, you might institute an "early warning system" whereby people reach out for help as soon as they realize they'll miss a deadline. You might also agree to regularly check in on the team's overall level of resources and to take action to replenish it when it's low.

Take the opportunity to reassess. Some things about your job are in your capacity to change; others are not. If, for example, the culture of your organization is characterized by pervasive incivility, it's unlikely that you'll ever thrive there. Or if the content of the work has no overlap with what you care about most, finding work that's more meaningful may be an essential step to thriving. There is no job that's worth your health, your sanity, or your soul. For many people, burnout is the lever that motivates them to pause, take stock, and create a career that's more satisfying than what they'd previously imagined.

Monique Valcour is a management academic, coach, and consultant.

CHAPTER 28

Pronouns Matter When Psyching Yourself Up

by Ozlem Ayduk and Ethan Kross

Some people seem to have an amazing ability to stay rational no matter what. They efficiently make good, clear decisions, while the rest of us waste energy doing things like panicking about upcoming tasks, ruminating pointlessly, or refusing to move on from our failures. Those cool-headed rationalists also seem adept at getting ahead, while we're mired in our all-too-human, biased habits of thinking. Could we ever become like them?

Adapted from content posted on hbr.org on February 6, 2015

The gulf between the two types of people seems vast and unbridgeable.

But it's not. It can be crossed, via a simple linguistic shift.

"You." Or "he." Or "she." Or even via your own name.

It's a matter of how you talk when you silently talk to yourself, as you probably do often, especially when you're confronted with a difficult task. Do you say something like "It's up to me"? Or "I can do it"? Or do you say "It's up to you" or address yourself by your own name?

Nobel Prize winner Malala Yousafzai demonstrated the use of the latter approach when she was asked by Jon Stewart how she felt upon finding out that she was on a Taliban hit list. She was fearful, but then she imagined how she'd respond if she was attacked: "I said, 'If he comes, what would you do, Malala?' . . . Then I would reply [to] myself, 'Malala, just take a shoe and hit him.'"

Does this shift from "I" to "Malala" represent a simple quirk of speech? Or does it reflect something deeper—a process that helped her manage the intense threat that confronted her?

We, along with seven of our colleagues—Jiyoung Park, Aleah Burson, Adrienne Dougherty, Holly Shablack, and Ryan Bremner of the University of Michigan; Jason Moser of Michigan State; and Emma Bruehlman-Senecal of UC Berkeley—recently addressed this question in a series of experiments. We found that cueing people to reflect on intense emotional experiences using their names and non-first-person pronouns such as "you" or "he" or "she" consistently helped them control their thoughts, feelings, and behaviors.

FIGURE 28-1

Pronouns matter when psyching yourself up

People who thought about themselves in the second or third person before giving a speech turned in better performances and ruminated less afterward than those who thought in the first person.

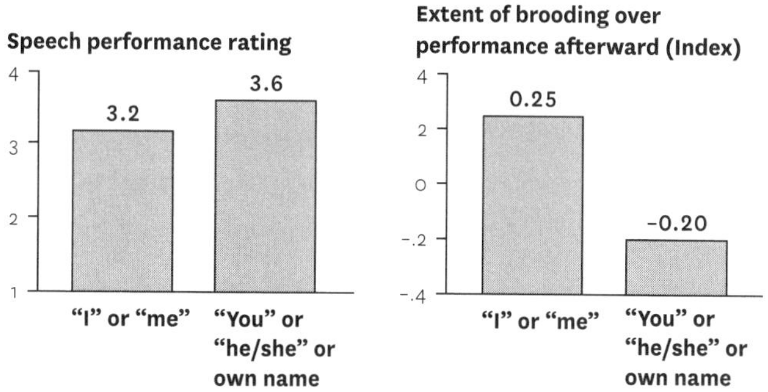

Source: Ethan Kross, Ozlem Ayduk, and the *Journal of Personality and Social Psychology*

For example, in one study we found that participants who silently referred to themselves in the second or third person or used their own names while preparing for a five-minute speech were calmer and more confident and performed better on the task than those who referred to themselves using "I" or "me." (See figure 28-1.)

The effects extended beyond the task, too: People who had used non-first-person pronouns or their names felt more positively about their performance on the speech once it was over. They also experienced less shame about it and ruminated about it less. Those are big pluses—ruminating endlessly over past experiences can hurt not only your psychological well-being but also your physical health.

It didn't matter whether the research subjects were anxious or calm at baseline; both types of people benefited from the subtle shift in language.

Nor were there different effects for use of the second- or third-person pronouns or their own names. All that mattered was whether the participants did or didn't use first-person pronouns.

It was impressive to see how a simple change in language could produce these effects. Having observed the power of this subtle shift, both of us now intentionally use it. One of us (Ozlem Ayduk) has even been known, when facing a difficult task, to write emails to herself using her name. The other (Ethan Kross) regularly prompts his five-year-old daughter to use her own name in thinking about why she feels distressed when she doesn't get her way.

Our findings are just a small part of a much larger, ongoing stream of research on self-talk, which is proving to have far-reaching implications for altering the way people think, feel, and behave. Not only does non-first-person self-talk help people perform better under stress and help them get control of their emotions, it also helps them reason more wisely.

Our past research indicates that a self-distancing effect can be achieved by cueing people to mentally adopt a "fly on the wall" perspective on their problems. Shifting visual perspective like that may work in situations where people have the time to reflect on experiences that have already occurred. What's exciting about the self-talk effects we found is that they lend themselves to real-time situations that are unfolding quickly. When you're in the midst of performing a task or interacting with others, the substitution of "you" for "I" can be done quickly and easily, and the results may surprise you.

Ozlem Ayduk is professor of psychology and director of the Relationships and Social Cognition Lab at the University of California Berkeley. **Ethan Kross** is professor of psychology and director of the Emotion and Self-Control Laboratory at the University of Michigan.

CHAPTER 29

Staying Motivated When Everyone Else Is on Vacation

by Dorie Clark

During vacation season, making even the slightest progress can seem like a Sisyphean task. You can't schedule that important meeting because the key players are on holiday. You have no idea where to find the data you need because your analytics staffers are off the grid. And you can't finalize the pitch deck because your boss isn't around to greenlight it. Being at work can seem pointless

Adapted from content posted on hbr.org on August 8, 2016

and frustrating when you're the only one trying to keep things on track.

For those times when it feels as if everyone else is out of the office, how can you stay motivated and actually make your time in the office count? Here are three approaches to keep in mind.

Embrace "Deep Work"

Georgetown computer science professor Cal Newport argues that "shallow work"—the brainless tasks that occupy our day, like responding to email—is often necessary to avoid getting fired. But, he says, the secret to attaining disproportionate professional success is our ability to engage in what he calls "deep work." With most of us sending and receiving an average of 122 emails per day, it can be hard to carve out space to work on meaningful tasks, like developing your go-to-market strategy or launching a new podcast. But when everyone else is on vacation, the level of inbound messages drops dramatically. You'll have more freedom to schedule uninterrupted blocks of time to tackle the important projects you've been putting off that could significantly benefit your career.

Clean Up Minor Tasks

If you're feeling too languid from the slower pace of an empty office to face the prospect of deep work, you could also make good use of your time by going in the opposite direction: devoting a day or two to clean up minor tasks that have been impeding your productivity throughout the year. We all have a list of projects that ought to be done, but never rise to the top of our to-do list. Perhaps it's cleaning off your desk, so you can find your files when you need them, instead of wasting minutes every day fumbling through a teetering stack. It could be handling those expense reports that accounting has been hounding you for, or writing a recommendation letter for your former intern, or updating your LinkedIn profile. Those tasks are never going to be as valuable as focused effort put toward your top strategic priorities. But they still need to be done, eventually. If you're feeling temporarily unmotivated, they'll give you a sense of accomplishment at the end of the day, as you wipe your slate of a legion of niggling to-dos.

Build Your Network

Networking is another task that many people consider important, but gets short shrift when work heats up. When many of your colleagues are out of the office, however, fewer people are expecting an immediate response to their messages, and no one is looking over your shoulder to see how long your lunch break is. So now may be the perfect time to reach out to other colleagues, inside or outside your organization. If they're also still in town, they may be more receptive than usual to your invitation to get together. Meet for coffee or linger over lunch, to solidify connections and gain new market insights that will make you more valuable to your colleagues when they return.

You can feel dispirited when every message you send is met with an autoresponder reminding you that you're the only one who's not on vacation. But the reward for holding down the fort is uninterrupted time to embrace meaningful work, to clear out the cobwebs that have been hindering your productivity, and to connect with colleagues and build a robust network. Those are all tasks we should embrace throughout the year, but too often we get caught in the hurly-burly of immediate demands.

Obviously, it's more fun if you're the one who's on vacation. But even if you're not, you can still reap the benefits of others taking time off.

Dorie Clark is a marketing strategist and professional speaker who teaches at Duke University's Fuqua School of Business. She is the author of *Reinventing You* (Harvard Business Review Press, 2013) and *Stand Out*, and the forthcoming *Entrepreneurial You* (Harvard Business Review Press, 2017). Learn more about her work at www.dorieclark.com.

SECTION FIVE

Get More Done on the Road

There's nothing like travel to interrupt any sort of productive workday rhythm you may have established in the office. But work doesn't stop just because you have to pack up and ship out somewhere.

This section of the guide will help you get more done when you're on the go.

CHAPTER 30

How to Use Your Travel Time Productively

by Dorie Clark

I'm writing this article on a flight to Raleigh-Durham; I began it last week on a train from New York City and added a few paragraphs a couple days later on a flight to San Francisco. I'm not alone: The Global Business Travel Association predicted that business travel spending would hit an all-time high of $1.25 trillion in 2015, a 6.5% increase over the previous year. Even in an era of video conferencing, face-to-face meetings are still an irreplaceable business tool, and many of us spend a majority of our time on the road.

Adapted from content posted on hbr.org on November 5, 2015

Of course, life doesn't stop when you're in the air: Emails continue to pour in, and reports and proposals are due no matter where you're sending them from. Even if it's a travel day, it's still a workday. But staying productive on the road—while navigating unfamiliar destinations, schlepping heavy luggage, and dealing with not-infrequent delays and inconveniences—can be a herculean challenge. Here's how to accomplish more while in transit.

Engage in professional development by **listening to podcasts**. Many airport rituals are short and staccato—5 minutes in line to check a bag, 10 minutes to get through security, 5 minutes walking to the gate, and 10 minutes standing in line to board. You certainly can't whip out a laptop and start typing while you're standing up and juggling your boarding pass and photo ID. Instead, podcasts are a perfect, hands-free way to mitigate your annoyance and learn something new. If a crackling loudspeaker interrupts your listening, you can easily rewind and replay what you missed. There are countless podcasts available on relevant professional topics, from legal issues to project management to entrepreneurship to marketing. HBR has its own weekly podcast as well.

If you have access to an airport lounge (where it's quieter), you can also use the time to **make a series of short phone calls**. Productivity expert David Allen, whom I profile in my book *Stand Out*, recommends keeping a "to call" list so that you can cluster the phone calls you need to make and bang them out in a row. Keith Ferrazzi, who writes frequently about networking, is also an advocate of short phone calls as a way of keeping your relationship alive with casual contacts. For instance, Facebook tracks your connections' birthdays; the thoughtful gesture of making a few quick birthday calls while you're waiting to board could make someone's day and cement your bond.

Though internet access is becoming more common on flights, it's still not a given. Even when Wi-Fi is offered, it can be slow or patchy. That's why I generally **focus on writing projects** that don't require use of the internet. I'll download all the necessary information and supporting materials beforehand, and then go offline to complete projects like writing articles, edits to book chapters, client reports, or interview questions I've committed to answer. The lack of internet access often enables me to focus better and avoid the distracting rabbit hole of online research that can delay my writing at the office.

And remember—as with everything—there's a balance. Numerous studies have touted the benefits of "strategic renewal." Instead of using *all* of your time on the plane to plow through reports or fine-tune a presentation deck, take some time for yourself. Do some **pleasure reading**—splurge on a magazine or a thriller at the airport newsstand (indeed, according to *Airport Revenue News*, the average passenger spends nearly $11 at the airport). Taking some downtime away from the grinding pace of work may enable you to be sharper once you get down to business.

Travel has become a standard part of many professionals' work life. This year, U.S. business travelers will make 488 million trips—about 1.3 million per day. With that much travel, we can't afford to write off days in transit; using that time wisely is essential to getting our jobs done. With these tips, you can ensure that a day on the road still moves your career forward.

Dorie Clark is a marketing strategist and professional speaker who teaches at Duke University's Fuqua School of Business. She is the author of *Reinventing You* (Harvard Business Review Press, 2013) and *Stand Out*, and the forthcoming *Entrepreneurial You* (Harvard Business Review Press, 2017). Learn more about her work at www.dorieclark.com.

CHAPTER 31

How to Get Work Done on the Road

by Joseph Grenny

One conversation 25 years ago changed business travel for me forever. My business partner, Kerry Patterson, and I were talking about a book we hoped to write. We had been yakking about it for a couple of years but had made no progress. Let me be more honest: *I* had made no progress. Kerry seemed to show up with reams of fascinating ideas written out in polished prose, while I had a stained airplane napkin with crayon drawings on it. I would mutter an apology for my paltry contribution but point to the 20 days I had been on the road the previous

Adapted from content posted on hbr.org on November 9, 2015

month. After many of these exchanges, Kerry looked at me and said, "Joseph, writers write."

His point hit me in the gut. It was clear that my career as a consultant would involve lots of travel and I had a choice about what I was going to do with that time. Since then, Kerry, our colleagues at VitalSmarts, and I have coauthored five books and hundreds of papers and articles, and developed dozens of best-selling training courses—all while I traveled over 100 days a year.

For me, the key to being productive while shuttling around the globe is to think of myself in the third person, as someone I need to carefully and deliberately influence. Here are the ways I do that—many of which I used to write this very article!

Make Appointments with Yourself

Behavioral economists have shown that making good choices is easy if you don't have to fulfill them *now*. If you ask me for a lunch order for next week, I'm likely to pick healthier choices than if I'm drooling over options I'll eat right now. The phenomenon is referred to as *hyperbolic discounting*—the tendency to overvalue rewards now and undervalue them later. This cognitive bias works in my favor when I trick myself into making commitments I will keep at a set time in the future. I am faithful to my calendar; if it says I am supposed to do something, I tend to do it. So I look ahead to big blocks of downtime during travel—for example, a five-hour plane trip from San Francisco to New York. This week I arrived at my hotel in Indianapolis, opened my calendar, and saw an entry I imposed on myself last week. From 4:30 to

5:00 p.m., the schedule demanded that I "Outline HBR article." So I did.

Stop Before You're Done

When I have long tasks to complete—ones that will require multiple work sessions—I'm careful to stop my work at a place that makes it easier (and more pleasant) for me to pick it up again later. For example, if I'm in a groove and have a story going that I'm enjoying writing, I intentionally stop before I finish it so I can look forward to jumping back in. The schedule entry above was a little piece of motivational trickery as well—notice that I only committed to "outline" this article. I find that I procrastinate most on this part of writing. But once I finish an outline, I savor fleshing out pieces of it. I limit my appointment to finish the hard piece, so that I feel enthusiastic about picking it up again later.

Create Satisfying Episodes

Psychologist Roy Baumeister has shown that your motivation is a finite resource. I find this to be especially true in the grind of business travel when my motivation is low. If I think of myself in the first person, I tend to be merciless, beating myself up for not getting anything done. When I think of myself in the third person, I tend to be more sympathetic of this limited resource. I ask, "How can I maximize Joseph's motivation?" Rather than forcing myself into a writing death march on a five-hour flight, I determine a portion of that task that would feel meaningful and satisfying to complete. For example, while boarding my Indiana flight, I thought, "If I can customize my presentation for tomorrow and empty my inbox, I will feel liberated." So that's what I did.

Feel the Endorphins

Busy people tend not to savor the endorphins that come with completing a task. Develop a habit of stopping and *feeling* the earned satisfaction from getting a block of work finished. Sit back in your seat on the plane or relax on your hotel bed, and take in the joy of having completed something difficult. Taking a moment like this creates new neural connections that associate productivity with pleasure rather than resentment.

Use the Power of the Notepad

The window of time when I first enter a hotel room is crucial for me. For years I noticed that my ritual was to find the TV remote and turn on CNN. Then I would set up my laptop and purchase the hotel Wi-Fi. While an avalanche of emails downloaded, I would begin moving into my closet and bathroom. Every time I followed this ritual, I would get sucked into something on the TV or my inbox that would sap my productivity. These days I use another trick on myself. I get an embarrassing amount of gratification out of putting a check in a box. So now when I enter my hotel room, I grab the free pad of paper on the desk and make a list of five things I want to get done before dinner. Then—and here's the not so high-tech part—I draw a little empty box next to each. That way, I feel compelled to get them done.

Reward Yourself

One of the reasons people lose their enthusiasm for being efficient and productive is that it can feel like a relentless grind—there's always more to do. Don't burn yourself out. If I have a long flight, I'll make some reasonable commitments to get things done, but I also allow time for relaxation and pleasure. Treat yourself as you would a valued employee—give lots of praise and encouragement for the great stuff you get done.

Business travel has been a boon to me over the past 30 years—a time when I've done some of my best work. It wouldn't have ended up that way, however, had Kerry not drawn my attention to the fact that I was using travel as an excuse rather than an opportunity.

Joseph Grenny is a four-time *New York Times* bestselling author, keynote speaker, and leading social scientist for business performance. His work has been translated into 28 languages, is available in 36 countries, and has generated results for 300 of the *Fortune* 500. He is the cofounder of VitalSmarts, an innovator in corporate training and leadership development.

SECTION SIX

Take Time Off

Sometimes taking a vacation hardly seems worth it. Before you go, you work extra hours trying to tackle what needs to be done. Once you're away, you may have to field urgent requests or deal with crises that emerge. And then you have to endure the post-vacation blues when you return to all of the work and messages that have piled up in your absence.

This section of the guide will help you prepare for and return from your vacation so that you're able to enjoy time away and ease back into your routine in a way that doesn't undo the positive effects of your time off.

CHAPTER 32

Going on Vacation Doesn't Have to Stress You Out at Work

by Elizabeth Grace Saunders

Vacations are the things that dreams and cruise commercials are made of. Ideally, you come back refreshed, recharged, and ready to go. But sometimes, the exact opposite is true. Who among us hasn't said at some point, usually the day before we leave, "Trying to take this vacation is so stressful, it would have been better not to go at all!" Sometimes vacation stress is unavoidable, but most times it's manageable if we prepare for it more

---

Adapted from content posted on hbr.org on June 2, 2015

strategically. As the owner of a time coaching and training company, I have found that many of my clients tell me that they were able to take their first really refreshing vacation in years by using the following strategies.

Initial Office Scheduling

One of the most important elements of reducing stress around your vacation is to decide well in advance when you'll take time off. This gives you the opportunity to protect the time before and after your holiday from too many commitments. It also gives you the ability to make thoughtful choices as you pull the details of your trip together. Having lead time reduces stress to such a degree that one of my clients who does high-end travel planning requires at least three months of advance notice.

Once you know that you want to take a vacation, immediately block out those dates on your calendar as "out of the office." It's best to not make plans for any scheduled items like conference calls while you're traveling. This way, the only work activities that you might end up doing during your vacation are the truly unexpected and urgent ones. Sure, you may have to check in on one or two things while you're away—life happens—but you should avoid having to do your regular work during your time out of the office.

Although you may be tempted to pack in as many meetings as you can before and after a trip, you'll end up feeling more relaxed if you create a buffer around your vacation. Schedule time a few days before you leave to wrap up projects, take care of important emails, and attend any truly urgent meetings. Reserve at least the first day that you return to the office to get your head back into work and clear out your inbox. It's the office equivalent of promptly getting your suitcases unpacked and your home in order instead of staying half unpacked for days or weeks on end.

Initial Travel Planning

How you structure your trip also has a significant impact on how refreshed you'll feel when you get back. I recommend taking at least a half day off of work before you leave to give yourself some margin for tackling any final packing details or errands. When you originally purchase your tickets, it's worth spending the extra money to travel at reasonable times. Having to get up at 3 a.m. to catch a flight will not put you in a good state of mind for your travels, and being sleep deprived makes it more likely that you'll get sick. And since you're planning well in advance, you'll find more affordable flights.

As you plan activities, don't just think about what you want to see or do; think about the sort of experience you want to have. Just because you're in Paris for the first time doesn't mean that you need to go to every museum on the map. You may find that you feel much happier—and more refreshed—by spending time at a few important spots and then giving yourself the luxury of sitting at a café for a few hours or taking a leisurely stroll.

If you're traveling with children, focus on simplicity, especially with very young kids, who are quite content with a pool to play in and a slower pace. Plan for everything to take longer than you'd expect, and relax into the fact that you're on vacation, so that's just fine.

The Week Before You Leave

At home: If you plan on taking a substantial vacation, start packing—or at least running errands—early. I find that blocking out time the weekend before the final week of work dramatically decreases the number of last-minute trips to the pharmacy or the dry cleaner.

At work: Coordinate with your colleagues so that everyone has clear expectations for what you will and won't be doing while you're out of the office. That could mean giving others the authority to make decisions on certain projects, or letting them know that in specific situations they should contact you.

Use your out-of-office message on your email and phone wisely. I like to state that I'm out of the office until X date and that I will return messages as promptly as possible after that time. That sets the expectation that I won't reply while on vacation and also that it may take a few days after I return to the office to reply. Additionally, if you start your out-of-office auto response a day before you actually leave, it'll be easier to extract yourself from the office on time, as you'll be able to focus on what's most essential during your last day in the office.

The Week You Return

To maximize the relaxing benefits of your vacation, have a good reentry plan. Arrive home a day early—or at least earlier in the day—so that you have some time to unpack, do laundry, and get a good night's sleep. Make a plan for the following day, so that you have a clear sense of how to approach your first day back in the office. Finally, instead of focusing on the fact that you're no longer on vacation, think about how grateful you are for the time you had away. Gratitude creates joy that can carry you through the initial shock of returning to "real life."

As you're planning your next getaway, make it truly refreshing by trying these strategies.

Elizabeth Grace Saunders is the author of *How to Invest Your Time Like Money* (Harvard Business Review Press, 2015), a time coach, and the founder of Real Life E Time Coaching & Training. Find out more at www.RealLifeE.com.

CHAPTER 33

Don't Obsess Over Getting Everything Done Before a Vacation

by Scott Edinger

Like most people, I find the week before a vacation to be something of a nightmare, as I attempt to clear the decks before I go. On the face of it, this seems like a good idea—get your work done (and ideally, the work you would have done during the time you'll be on vacation), and you can go off with your mind at rest. But I believe I've been thinking about this entirely backward.

Adapted from content posted on hbr.org on June 9, 2015

Far from freeing you to enjoy that time away, what's really happening is that you're stealing energy from the future to clear the decks, and as a result turning your relaxation time into recuperation time. I need only go back to the last vacation I took to demonstrate this point. See if this sounds familiar: I was working on some deadlines (self-imposed, of course), and for three days leading up to our departure, I put in significantly more time and energy than usual. I stayed up very late the night before leaving, working until the early morning hours. Caffeine and excitement helped me get moving, but by mid-afternoon, I was toast. It took several days to make up the sleep deficit, and I missed out on having fun with my family while I got that extra sleep. Three days of a weeklong vacation is no small percentage. Worse, I know I was far less attentive and focused those first few days away than I typically am. I certainly didn't maximize that precious and important time away from work.

How can you avoid making the same mistakes I did?

Maintain Your Regular Schedule Before Your Vacation

I'm not suggesting you need to be a slacker, but too many of us overdo it to get work done just before a holiday, thinking that we'll make up for it with rest during our time off. That's a mistake. So, as much as you can, try to make the week leading up to vacation a typical one in terms of the energy you expend or hours you put in. For those of you who say "I run hard all the time," consider the difference between high speed and your maximum.

Check In on Vacation

It's not entirely necessary to completely unplug from work while you're on vacation. There are vacation purists who believe that any kind of attention to work during a vacation is a violation of one's time to recharge. Then there are those who believe it's okay to occasionally screen email for critical issues. Is there some sort of constructive compromise?

When you succumb to the seemingly sensible notion of stealing the odd moment of vacation downtime to slip in some work, your mind is as far away as it would be if you were physically in the office, as all of your companions are acutely aware. If you doubt this, picture your spouse or your children sitting at dinner with eyes cast down at their cell phones just at the moment some intriguing, surprising, or funny notion pops into your head that you want to share.

So, the idea is not to forbid contact with work but to establish clear ground rules about when you will engage in it, with the explicit recognition that when you're engaged in work, you really aren't on vacation. There's no right way to do this, but here's my rule of thumb: During a weeklong vacation, take at least 72 consecutive hours with no work, no email, and—if you are daring—no screens. For longer vacations, adjust the time accordingly or oscillate between the two. Then only spend 30 to 60 minutes a day quickly checking in on truly urgent issues. This allows you to be unplugged for the remainder of the day.

When I tried this, I experienced a major epiphany about how much checking my email on my phone is reflex rather than need. I asked my 11-year-old to take my phone and only give it to me when we needed to check something online related to one of our trivia games or vacation plans. I was shocked to see how often I reached for my phone, entirely out of habit rather than necessity. I reminded myself in those embarrassingly frequent moments to look up, take a breath, and notice something happening around me. As I became more fully engaged in the real world, I discovered I really liked the feeling of not having my phone for a few days. It is decidedly liberating. And when I returned to my phone on check-in days, I found it easier to avoid being sucked in by email.

Accept That Work Will Be Fine Without You

To be able to truly go on vacation, convince yourself that the world can do without you during that time. This is at once self-evident, critical, and very difficult to accept. I'm not saying you don't make a difference, or even that you won't be missed. But I am suggesting any negative impact will be modest and quickly ameliorated upon your return.

I own my own business, so the stakes for its success could not be higher for both me and my family. But even so, some of the so-called "urgency" I've created isn't urgent at all. Most deadlines or expectations with clients, staffers, and myself can be negotiated. One of my clients said to me a few months ago, "I don't really have the time to take this vacation." If you're nodding your head here, that's a clue that you need to take a step back and realistically think through your concerns. I find making them physically concrete, by actually making a list of your concerns, can help. Then consider the impact and the worst possible consequences of each. I expect you'll see they're rarely unrecoverable. Add to that the likelihood of anything occurring at its most severe level, and you'll be thinking clearly and see that it is possible to take time off.

If it makes you feel better, take your peers, direct reports, and perhaps even your boss through the same thought process. Ask them to consider the implications of your time off and think through the probable scenarios, as well as the odds of their happening. For many of us, our work is such a vital part of our lives that we have a distorted view of our own importance. When we step back and change our perspective, we give ourselves permission to not be indispensable for a time. Odds are, the world will be okay if you're out for a week or so.

Invest wisely in your time off through preparation, shifting your mindset, and limiting your engagement with what's going on back at the office, and you can expect to accomplish great things when you return, truly rejuvenated.

Scott Edinger is the founder of Edinger Consulting Group. He is a coauthor of the HBR article "Making Yourself Indispensable." His latest book is *The Hidden Leader: Discover and Develop Greatness Within Your Company*. Follow him on Twitter: @ScottKEdinger.

CHAPTER 34

Ease the Pain of Returning to Work After Time Off

by Alexandra Samuel

As much as we all need a break, the day or week *after* some time off often leaves us wondering whether the joy of vacation is worth the pain of returning to work. Between the email backlog, the pain of readjustment, and the fight to fit into your work clothes after two weeks of eating *all* the biscuits in Oregon (strictly hypothetically), you may feel as if you need another vacation just to recover from the stress of getting into a work groove. But a simple set of digital tools and practices can make

---

Adapted from content posted on hbr.org on June 8, 2015

it easier to get your work mojo back—particularly if you lay the groundwork before your vacation.

Before Your Vacation

Triage and queue your tasks

Use the week before your annual or semiannual vacation to ruthlessly cull your task list: Now is the time to move all those hazy or long-neglected to-dos out of your main task list and into a "someday/maybe/never" list.

Make a short priority list of what you actually need or want to tackle in the week or two after vacation, and annotate that list with where you'll start with each one. (I like to put that list in a digital notebook like Evernote, but you could put it on Google Drive or even a Word document.)

Set up timed alerts that will remind you at a specific date and time of any task that *must* get addressed that first week back, in case it takes you a day or two to feel up to looking at your task list.

Along with your list of key priorities, make a separate list of interesting or easy tasks you can tackle in week one, so you can knock off some fun stuff while you're waiting for your work brain to turn back on.

Park on a downhill slope

A common bit of wisdom on writing is to "park on a downhill slope": Wrap up your day's writing by leaving yourself a note about where you intend to pick up the next day. It's actually easier to take the next step of a project that's already underway than to start from a blank page, so "park" at least a couple of projects on a downhill slope by writing yourself a note about where to begin on your return.

If you're choosing which projects to wrap up before vacation and which to leave for completion upon your return, leave the most enjoyable or interesting challenges unfinished—that way you'll have something to look forward to when you get back. Put together a folder of emails or a project-related notebook in Evernote to help you get your work underway as easily as possible.

Lower expectations for your return

Give yourself a little margin for getting back into the flow of online communications by setting expectations with your pre-vacation messages. When you set up your out-of-office reply, tell people you'll be back on email a couple of days after you're returning from vacation; my vacation message always tells people that while I'll try to work my way through the backlog, I can't guarantee it, so they should email again after X date if they need a response.

Also give yourself a little wiggle room for your return to any social networks you participate in regularly; whether you're prescheduling social media updates (with a tool like Hootsuite or Buffer) for your vacation, or simply telling people that you're going dark while you're away, allow yourself an extra three to seven days before you plan on resuming your usual social network posting schedule.

Plan for your first week back

Block off significant chunks of time in your calendar for the week you get back so that you don't return to five days of back-to-back meetings. Just as important, schedule a couple of lunch or coffee dates with people you'll enjoy seeing, so that you have something to look forward to.

When You Return

Stay in stealth mode

Leave your email responder on for an extra day or two, so your colleagues and clients don't expect an instant response. In the same vein, stay off the intra-office chat network, and either avoid other in-house and external social networks (like Slack, Yammer, Twitter, and LinkedIn) or limit your participation to one or two short windows a day. Leave Skype and other chat systems in "do not disturb" mode and the ringer off on your phone. The one exception: Consider choosing one channel (like Google Chat or Facebook Messenger) that you'll use to reconnect with family, friends, and maybe one or two favorite colleagues.

Make work fun

Put your first week back to good use by doing neglected tasks you actually enjoy. I'm a productivity nerd, so (surprise!) my idea of fun is cleaning up my tech setup and adding to or improving the productivity tools in my toolkit. (The Apple app store always enjoys a little revenue bump the week I come back from vacation.)

Use technology to distract yourself

I know, I know: Digital distraction is unhealthy. But here's one time when it can really work *for* you, by taking your mind off the suffering of being back at work. When you're working alone at your desk, use a new Spotify playlist to entertain yourself while you catch up on mundane tasks. When you go to a meeting (especially one you're dreading), leave your phone on and allow yourself the luxury of intermittently peeking at Twitter, Flipboard, or whatever else will keep you from standing up and doing a Don Draper–style walkout.

And if you find yourself desperate to just chuck it all, put a date in your calendar for three to six weeks from now with a timed alert, saying "consider quitting my job"—and then put it out of your mind until the alert pops up. The odds are good that you'll be back in the swing of things by then, and if not . . . well, you probably *should* start thinking about your exit plan.

Even if you experience some residual vacation hangover, remember that's not necessarily a bad thing: It's more likely to be a sign that you've done a really great job of unplugging from work than a sign that you've returned to the wrong job. Use your tech setup to minimize the pain of the transition back to work, and you'll maximize the restorative effects of the vacation itself.

Alexandra Samuel is a speaker, researcher, and writer who works with the world's leading companies to understand their online customers and craft data-driven reports like "Sharing Is the New Buying." The author of *Work Smarter with Social Media* (Harvard Business Review Press, 2015), Alex holds a PhD in political science from Harvard University. Follow her on Twitter: @awsamuel.

Index

ABC method, and focus, 114
accomplishment(s)
  acknowledging your, and motivation, 149
  meaning from, 166
  reduced personal, and burnout, 182
action
  hidden blockages to, 179
  making benefits of feel bigger, 176–177
  making costs of feel smaller, 178–179
  See also procrastination
agency, and meaning at work, 167
amygdala, 112. *See also* brain
anxiety, 107. *See also* distractions
appointment, with yourself, 204–205. *See also* planning
arrangers, 30. *See also* productivity styles
assessments, self, 9–10, 18–19, 25–28
attention, building your, 108–109
attention economy, 127–128. *See also* focus
authenticity, and managing your stress, 21
autonomy, and meaning at work, 167–168
awareness, 129. *See also* mindfulness

belonging, to a community, and meaning at work, 167
boundaries, work-life, 91, 147–148, 151–152
brain
  neuroimaging of, 112
  physical breaks and, 114–115
  training to focus, 111–115
breaks
  helping others during, 100
  to look at nature, 139–144
  microbreaks, 131–137, 142–143
  physical, 109, 114–115
  set-shifting, 114–115
  walking, 109, 134
  working from home and, 148
breathing exercises, 128. *See also* mindfulness

buffers, 120–121. *See also* focus
burnout, 120, 135, 181–186

calendar
  adding commitments to, 69
  reviewing your, 66
  software, and working remotely, 154–155
  See also planning
cleanliness, 119–120, 126. *See also* focus; willpower
clutter, 119–120. *See also* focus; willpower
coffee breaks, 131–137. *See also* breaks
collaboration tools, 30, 154
colleagues, time wasting, 85–89
commitments
  adjusting, 66, 68–69
  saying no to, 65, 71–78
  too many, 63–69
  to yourself, 204–205
community, belonging to, and meaning at work, 167
commute time, 108–109, 129
contributions, beyond yourself, and meaning at work, 164–165
control, and managing your stress, 20–21
conversation, having a difficult, 88–89. *See also* colleagues, time wasting

deep work, 194. *See also* planning
delegation, of tasks, 3–4, 7, 9–11
depersonalization, 182. *See also* burnout
detachment, 136. *See also* work-life boundary
digital devices, 117, 220, 226–227
distractions
  ability to focus and, 117–118
  in meetings, 111
  minimizing, 105–109, 113–114
  succumbing to, 103
  willpower in face of, 123–126
document collaboration software, 154
downtime, 125–126. *See also* willpower

email, 87, 88, 106, 194
emotional exhaustion, 182. *See also* burnout
emotional vocabulary, 84. *See also* emotions
emotion management, 82–84
emotions
  monitoring, 107
  negative, 112–113
  positive, 112–113
endorphins, and task completion, 206
executive function, 115. *See also* brain
exercise, 83, 124

focus
  challenges destroying ability to, 117–121
  finding, 103
  looking at nature and, 139–144
  microbreaks and, 131–137
  mindfulness and, 127–130
  minimizing distractions and, 105–109, 113–114

time and space for, 108
training brain to, 111–115
free time, 66, 67–68. *See also* planning
frenzy, 112–113. *See also* brain; emotions
front-loading, 94–95. *See also* planning

goals
aligning time management with, 47–51
if-then planning to reach, 53–55
listing, 48
monitoring, 125
new requests and existing, 77–78
sprints and, 57–61

habit building, and willpower, 124–125
hardware, for remote work, 156–157
high performance, time for, 42. *See also* planning

if-then planning, 53–55, 173–174
inaction, downside of, 177
instant messaging, and working remotely, 155
internal voice. *See* self-talk
interruptions, managing, 93–94, 105–109
isolation, managing, 148–149, 150–151, 158. *See also* working from home

job resources, increasing to avoid burnout, 185–186. *See also* burnout
job stressors, reducing, 185. *See also* burnout

knowledge workers
challenge of managing, 5
time management for, 3–13
work of, 5–7

learning, and meaning at work, 165–166
lists, making, 206. *See also* tasks
low-complexity tasks, 107. *See also* tasks
low-value tasks, 3–13. *See also* tasks

meaning making, at work, 163–168
meditation, 118–119
meetings
distractions in, 111
in-person, 88
shrinking, 120
time between, 67–68, 119, 120–121
time spent on, 5, 7, 93, 118, 119
microbreaks, 131–137, 142–143
mindfulness, 83–84, 118–119, 127–130
mindset, 83. *See also* emotions
minor tasks, 194–195. *See also* tasks
monitoring progress, and willpower, 125. *See also* willpower

motivation, 161, 163–196
as finite resource, 205
during vacation season, 193–196
when working from home, 149
multitasking, 111, 119. *See also* focus

nature, looking at, 139–144
neatness, 126. *See also* cleanliness; clutter
negative emotions, 112–113. *See also* emotions
negative feedback, when saying no, 74–75. *See also* planning
networking, 195–196
note sharing software, and working remotely, 154

overcommitment, 63–69. *See also* planning
overwork, 91–95. *See also* work-life boundary

pauses, creating before committing, 65
performance, stress and, 15–17
personal growth, 165–166
personal productivity style, 25–31
phone calls, 87, 88, 200–201
physical breaks, 109, 114–115, 134. *See also* breaks
physical health, 83, 184
planners, 29–30. *See also* productivity styles
planning
benefits of, 35–39
if-then, 53–55, 173–174
pain of, 36–37
time for, 37–38
work at home schedule, 146–148, 150
positive emotions, 112–113. *See also* emotions
power, and meaning at work, 166
present bias, 176. *See also* procrastination
prestige, and meaning at work, 166. *See also* meaning making, at work
prevention focus, 170–171. *See also* motivation
prioritization, of tasks, 3–13, 42–44, 80–81
prioritizers, 28–29. *See also* productivity styles
procrastination, 100, 169–174, 175–179
productivity apps, 29
productivity styles, 25–31
productivity tools, 28–31
projects
saying no to new, 65, 71–78
thinking through new, 65–66. *See also* planning
promotion focus, 170–171. *See also* motivation
pronouns, use of in self-talk, 187–191
psychological detachment, 136. *See also* work-life boundary
purpose, and meaning at work, 164–165. *See also* meaning making, at work

remote work
best practices, 157–158
tools for, 153–158
See also working from home

responsibilities, reducing number of, 63–69. *See also* planning
rewards, for yourself, 207. *See also* motivation
rituals, and managing your stress, 21–22

saying no, 65, 71–78
schedules
  calendaring software for, 154–155
  gaps in, 67–68
  for vacations, 212–214
  work at home, 146–148, 150, 158
screen sharing software, and working remotely, 155
self-assessments, 9–10, 18–19, 25–28
self-care, 95, 125–126, 184
self-control, 123–126, 173
self-monitoring, and willpower, 125
self-realization, and meaning at work, 165–166. *See also* meaning making, at work
self-talk, 187–191, 205–206
set-shifting, 114–115. *See also* focus
shift sets, 114–115. *See also* focus
slow time, 41–46. *See also* planning
social connections, and working remotely, 158
social networks, and working remotely, 155–156
social purpose, and meaning at work, 167–168. *See also* meaning making, at work
software, for remote work, 154–156
solitude, and focus, 108
sprints, and project planning, 57–61
Start/Stop/Continue exercise, 8
status, and meaning at work, 166
stress, 15–22, 72, 91, 92, 185, 211–212
stress hormones, 128. *See also* physical health

tasks
  administrative, 49
  anxiety over, 107
  delegating, 3–4, 9–11
  eliminating unimportant, 3–4, 7, 9–11
  listing, 206
  logging your, 50–51
  low-complexity, 107
  low-value, 3–13
  minor, 194–195
  organizing, 119
  prioritizing, 3–13, 42–46, 80–81
  stopping mid, 205
  triaging, 81–84
  unimportant, 44
telecommuting
  effective, 145–152
  tools for, 153–158
third person, and self-talk, 205–206. *See also* self-talk
time
  allocation, 11–12
  buffer, 120–121
  demands on, 79–84
  free, 66, 67–68
  for planning, 37–38
  to replenish, 125–126

time (*continued*)
slow, 41–46
spent helping others, 97–101
tracking your, 48–51, 184
wasters, 85–89
time management
aligning with goals, 47–51
task prioritization and, 3–13, 42–46
work hours and, 91–95
travel
using productively, 197, 199–202, 203–207
See also vacations
triage, 81–84. *See also* prioritization, of tasks

vacations, 209
checking in during, 219–220
motivation while others are on, 193–196
preparing for, 212–214, 217–221, 224–226
returning from, 214–215, 223–227
stress and, 211–212
well-being and, 135–136
visualizers, 30–31. *See also* productivity styles

walking, 109, 134. *See also* breaks
willpower, 123–126, 173
work
"deep," 194
finding meaning at, 163–168
overcoming procrastination at, 169–174, 175–179
pace of, 41–46
purpose of, 164–165
reassessing your, 186
stopping, 205
time spent on, 163
work commitments. *See* commitments
workday
end of, 92
length of, 136
work environment, cleanliness of, 119–120, 126. *See also* focus
work hours, 91–95, 150
working from home
being effective while, 145–152
best practices, 157–158
examples of, 149–152
isolation of, 148–149, 150–151, 158
scheduling time when, 146–148, 150, 158
tools for, 153–158
work-life boundary, 91, 147–148, 151–152
work overload, 91–95, 182
work routines, 172. *See also* willpower

Yerkes-Dodson law, 16–17. *See also* stress

Notes

Notes

Notes

Notes

Notes

Notes

Notes